高职高专旅游类专业精品教材

酒店实用英语
基础会话篇

ENGLISH FOR HOTEL STAFF | BASIC COMMUNICATION

张 茵 主编　夏月梅 副主编

U0360710

清华大学出版社
北京

内 容 简 介

　　《酒店实用英语(基础会话篇)》针对酒店英语初级学习者编写。本系列教材内容体系以实际工作流程为导向,让学生自然融入真实情境,实现掌握职业英语的目的。同时贯彻党的二十大精神,巧妙融入中国特色思政元素,真正让学习入脑入心。本书紧扣《酒店运营管理职业技能等级证书》,共有6个模块、20个主题情境和60个子任务;学习内容以完成任务、解决问题入手,侧重听说训练及课堂小组讨论,配有课件和音频二维码,体现职业性、实用性、趣味性和时代感。既适合高职高专酒店管理专业学生的实践教学使用,也可作为酒店行业一线员工培训教材和自学读本,还适合"一带一路"沿线国家在华留学生的酒店管理课程使用。

图书在版编目(CIP)数据

　　酒店实用英语 . 基础会话篇 / 张茵主编 . — 北京:清华大学出版社,2017(2024.9 重印)
(高职高专旅游类专业精品教材)

　　ISBN 978-7-302-47340-4

　　Ⅰ . ①酒⋯　Ⅱ . ①张⋯　Ⅲ . ①饭店 – 英语 – 高等职业教育 – 教材　Ⅳ . ① F719.3

　　中国版本图书馆 CIP 数据核字(2017)第 124097 号

责任编辑: 王如月　周　菁
封面设计: 常雪影
责任校对: 王凤芝
责任印制: 刘　菲

出版发行: 清华大学出版社
　　　　　　网　　　址: https://www.tup.com.cn,https://www.wqxuetang.com
　　　　　　地　　　址: 北京清华大学学研大厦 A 座　　　　　　邮　　编: 100084
　　　　　　社 总 机: 010-83470000　　　　　　　　　　　　邮　　购: 010-62786544
　　　　　　投稿与读者服务: 010-62776969,c-service@tup.tsinghua.edu.cn
　　　　　　质量反馈: 010-62772015,zhiliang@tup.tsinghua.edu.cn

印 装 者: 涿州汇美亿浓印刷有限公司
经　　销: 全国新华书店
开　　本: 210mm×285mm　　　　**印　　张:** 15.25　　　　**字　　数:** 271 千字
版　　次: 2017 年 12 月第 1 版　　　　　　　　　　　　　**印　　次:** 2024 年 9 月第 7 次印刷
定　　价: 99.00 元

产品编号: 062053-03

本书编委会

主　编：张　茵

副主编：夏月梅

成　员（以姓氏拼音为序）

是　静　宋长来　陶玉婷　王　玲　王贺玲　吴　敏

辛衍君　徐　沁　徐　岩　颜　君　尹　奎　张秀芹

郑国中　周　丽

中国作为世界旅游板块的亚太核心，正在发挥越来越重要的作用。《中华人民共和国国民经济和社会发展第十四个五年规划和2035年远景目标纲要》中有多处提到旅游产业发展，包括"加快发展健康、养老、托育、文化、旅游、体育、物业等服务业""推动购物消费、居家生活、旅游休闲、交通出行等各类场景数字化，打造智慧共享、和睦共治的新型数字生活""深入发展大众旅游、智慧旅游，创新旅游产品体系，改善旅游消费体验""推动文化和旅游融合发展"等，足见政府对旅游业升级发展的持续关注。党的二十大报告中提及的"坚持以文塑旅、以旅彰文，推进文化和旅游深度融合发展"，"深入实施科教兴国战略、人才强国战略、创新驱动发展战略"等，坚持为党育人、为国育才，体现了未来旅游市场的广阔前景以及对行业人才的高标准要求。

随着中国文化自信、中国文化走出去，旅游业作为开放性、综合性产业，在共建"一带一路"战略中发挥着独特优势。现代旅游服务行业的岗位对旅游从业人员的对外服务能力提出了更高的要求。《教育部关于加强高职高专教人才培养工作的意见》中明确提出：高职高专教育"以适应社会需要为目标、以培养技术应用能力为主线设计学生的知识、能力、素质结构和培养方案，毕业生应具有基础理论知识适度、技术应用能力强、知识面较宽、素质高等特点""课程和教学内容体系改革是高职高专教学改革的重点和难点"。

《酒店实用英语（基础会话篇）》和《酒店实用英语（灵活运用篇）》是站在国家职业教育与人才培养的战略高度，密切结合国家人才培养的价值引领和高校课程思政建设的战略意义，响应"一带一路"国家战略需要，结合高职教育的国内外优秀专业师资（同时具有教学经验与行业经验）、行业专家的指导意见与行业标准、精心打造出版的一系列通用酒店服务行业英语教材。

一、教材特色

本套教材主要有以下特色：

巧妙融入课程思政，信息时代"活学活用"。本教材在编写过程中与时俱进，教学内容融入中国特色的思政元素，培养学生语用理解和表达能力，提高文化语境意识，培养学生的"家国情怀"和"世界眼光"；补充现代酒店服务的新流程，包括目前流行的网络预订、快捷支付、机器人送餐等环节。书中每个模块都有一个二维码，读者直接扫描就可以在移动终端上收听相关的音频和对话信息，随时

PREFACE

随地学习、掌握。

以行业证书为标准，满足不同学生实际需要。本教材依据《国家餐饮服务师职业资格考试》《国家客房服务师资格考试》和《酒店运营管理职业技能等级证书》中关于英语语言的使用标准和要求，设计内容和难度，分为基础会话和灵活运用两个部分。该教材以职业活动为导向，建立以职业功能为主线、主题情境为载体、工作任务为驱动的学习方式，结合职业资格证书（技能证书）制度与高职学历教育的有机结合（即"融通"），满足不同水平学生的实际需求。

还原工作本来面貌，以实际工作流程为导向。本教材依据真实职业岗位工作流程精心设计主题情境，教材内容与职业标准对接，每个主题情境下设若干具体的小任务。教材设计以酒店各部门工作场所为载体，两个级别共包括 12 个模块、40 个主题学习情境和 120 个工作任务，基本上涵盖了酒店服务的各个环节。通过细化工作任务，确保教学内容真实有效，提高教学内容针对性及职业岗位能力培养适用性。侧重选择过程完整、相对独立的工作任务，使学生在完成任务的过程中形成解决实际问题的能力。

二、教材结构

以《酒店实用英语（基础会话篇）》为例，全书共有 6 个模块，20 个主题情境，60 个子任务。课文所有学习内容均以完成任务、解决问题入手，侧重听说训练及课堂小组讨论，没有堆砌大量对话。对话文本在附录中体现，更侧重知识的实际运用性、趣味性和可操作性。整本教材结构如下：

（1）全书以酒店实际工作内容来设计教学内容，分为酒店概述、前厅服务、客房服务、餐饮服务、商务中心服务、特殊服务 6 个模块。

（2）每个模块分别设置不同的主题情境，每个主题情境都设有任务目标，其目的是使教师和学生能在任务开始前掌握本情境的教学重点。

（3）Introduction：每个主题情境通过其部门功能介绍引入学习任务，其目的是使教师和学生对该部门工作职能再次加深了解。

（4）Brainstorm：头脑风暴，通过讨论回忆并总结基础会话部分所学过并掌握的词汇及表达，为本模块知识的引入和掌握起到铺垫作用。

（5）Tasks：每个主题情境根据具体职业要求分为 3~4 个子任务，学习内容从解决问题入手，总结子任务中常见短语和句子表达，随即进行有针对性的练习，便于学生迅速掌握相关知识和技能。

（6）Vocabulary：提供酒店场景对话中常用的英语词汇，便于学生校音记忆。

（7）Exercise：提供实务场景资料，通过翻译、口译、讨论、阅读等练习，帮助学生更有效地掌握语言运用及职业技能。

（8）Tips：提供相关语言使用贴士或者行业小短文，开阔视野，供学有余力的学生使用。

（9）Dialogue-Scripts：展示本书所有主题情境对话原稿，帮助学生课前预习或课后复习总结。

（10）Appendix：附录部分提供补充资料，包括酒店管理人员岗位名称、餐饮常用词汇，方便学生学习和工作中查询使用。

三、教材使用说明

本套教材的主编根据其多年教研经验和在酒店一线工作的经历，结合自己在加拿大和美国访学期间阅读的大量外版书，在教材内容的设计上鼓励学生探讨式学习、注重培养学生的思维创新能力。教材编写者均为长期从事酒店经营管理专业教学并具有一线经验的专业教师：第一、二、四部分及附录由常州工业职业技术学院的张茵老师编写，第三、五、六部分由常州工业职业技术学院的夏月梅老师编写。

书中我们还专门为授课教师提供了《酒店服务英语教学参考大纲》，教师可参考大纲内的课时数安排进行教学、也可根据教学实际情况进行课时数的调整。此外，每册教材均配有教学课件和二维码扫码收听语音功能，方便教师授课使用。本系列教材既适合高职高专酒店管理专业学生学习使用，也可作为酒店行业培训教材和酒店从业人员的自学教材。本教材为全英文教材，也适用于"一带一路"沿线国家在华留学生的酒店管理课程使用。

教材成稿之后，我们还广泛听取了国内外酒店英语教育专家和国际酒店业高管的意见和建议。教材的编写凝聚了诸多专家学者的经验和智慧。在此，对为本套教材的编写和出版付出辛勤劳动的所有老师、行业专家及出版社的各位老师表示衷心的感谢。特别要感谢常州新城希尔顿酒店和江苏凤凰台饭店集团有限公司的大力支持，本书图片由其授权许可使用。由于编写能力和编写时间有限，疏漏之处在所难免，恳请广大读者和专家批评指正。

编者写于2023年夏

酒店服务英语参考大纲
（基础会话篇）

（**课时建议**：42学时，注重单个服务环节的细节流程，英语语言的基础交流）

序号	学习情境	工 作 任 务	学时
模块一	**Introduction to Hotels　酒店概述**		**2课时**
1-1	Getting to Know Hotels 初识酒店	Hotel Types，Hotel Rating，Selection Tips 酒店分类；酒店等级；选择建议	2
模块二	**The Front Desk　前厅服务英语**		**10课时**
2-1	Room Reservations 客房预订	Room Type, Room Rate, Receiving Room Reservations 房间类型；房价；接待客房预订	2
2-2	Bellman Service 行李员服务	Receiving Guests, Introducing Services, Luggage Delivery 迎接客人；介绍酒店服务；行李入房	2
2-3	Check-in 登记入住	Check-in with Reservation, Walk-in Guest Service, No Rooms Available 有预订客人；无预订客人；酒店客满	2
2-4	At Information Desk 问询服务	Lost & Found, Giving Directions, Leaving a Message 失物招领；指引方向；代客留言	2
2-5	Check-out 结账离开	Payment Options, Bill Explanation, Express Check-out 结账类型；账单说明;快速结账	2
模块三	**Housekeeping Department　客房服务英语**		**6课时**
3-1	Receiving Guests 迎宾服务	Guiding Guests to Their Rooms, Introducing the Room Facilities, Answering Questions 引客进房；介绍房间设施；回答客人问题	2
3-2	Chamber Service 客房服务	Cleaning the Room, Asking for Extra Items (Adding Items), DND Service 整理房间；添加用品；请勿打扰	2
3-3	Laundry Service 洗衣服务	How to Get the Service, Filling in the Laundry List, Delivering the Wrong Laundry 介绍洗衣服务；填写洗衣单；送错衣服	2

序号	学习情境	工 作 任 务	学时
模块四	**Food & Beverage Department　餐饮服务英语**		**10课时**
4-1	Table Reservations 预订餐台	Receiving Reservations, Changing Reservations, Fully Booked 接受预订；更改预订；餐厅订满	2
4-2	Greeting Guests 迎客服务	Receiving Guests, Seating Guests, No Seats Available 迎接客人；安排入座；餐位已满	2
4-3	Taking Orders 点菜服务	Presenting Menus, Today's Special, Making Recommendations 点菜咨询；特色菜肴；提供建议	2
4-4	Serving Dishes 席间服务	Describing Dishes, Offering Help, Asking for Opinions 介绍菜品；提供帮助；询问用餐意见	2
4-5	Wine Service 酒水服务	Chinese Wine, Western Wine, Serving Wine 中式酒水；西式酒水；斟酒服务	2
模块五	**Business Center　商务中心服务英语**		**6课时**
5-1	General Switchboard 通信服务	Leaving a Message, Waking-up Call Service, IDD System 电话留言；叫醒服务；国际长途电话直拨	2
5-2	Secretarial Services 文秘服务	Photocopying, Sending Fax, Booking Tickets 复印服务；收发传真；订票	2
5-3	Providing Information 提供信息	Sightseeing Suggestions, Answering Questions, Delivery Service 观光指导；咨询信息；邮寄服务	2
模块六	**Special Services　特殊服务英语**		**6课时**
6-1	Recreation Service 康乐服务	Introducing Facilities, Giving Suggestions, Shopping Center 设施介绍；应对需求；购物中心	2
6-2	At the Cloakroom 寄存服务	Luggage Storage, Luggage Pick-up, Valuables Storage 行李寄存；行李提取；贵重物品寄存	2
6-3	Handling Complaints 处理投诉	Receiving Complaints, Apologizing to Guests, Asking for Help 接受投诉；致歉；寻求帮忙	2

目　录

Part 1 Introduction to Hotels

1

| Scene One | Getting to Know Hotels | 2 |

Part 2 The Front Desk

11

Scene One	Room Reservations	12
Scene Two	Bellman Service	19
Scene Three	Check-in	26
Scene Four	At Information Desk	34
Scene Five	Check-out	41

Part 3 Housekeeping Department

49

Scene One	Receiving Guests	50
Scene Two	Chamber Service	57
Scene Three	Laundry Service	63

CONTENTS

Part 4 Food & Beverage Department 71

Scene One	Table Reservations	**72**
Scene Two	Greeting Guests	**78**
Scene Three	Taking Orders	**85**
Scene Four	Serving Dishes	**92**
Scene Five	Wine Service	**99**

Part 5 Business Center 107

Scene One	General Switchboard	**108**
Scene Two	Secretarial Services	**116**
Scene Three	Providing Information	**124**

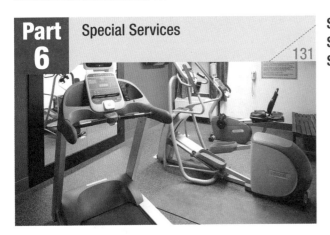

Part 6 Special Services 131

Scene One	Recreation Service	**132**
Scene Two	At the Cloakroom	**139**
Scene Three	Handling Complaints	**146**

目   录

Dialogue-Scripts & Reference Answer   153

Appendix I: Hotel Management Organization   224

Appendix II:Food & Beverage Vocabulary   226

参考文献   229

Part 1

Introduction to Hotels
酒店概述

Introduction to Hotels
酒店概述

A hotel is an establishment that provides lodging, meals, and other guest services, like business center, childcare, meeting rooms, stores, swimming pools, and etc. Different hotels meet the different needs of the customers.

There are usually management employees, maintenance employees, kitchen and wait staff (if the hotel has a restaurant), housekeeping staff members, front desk employees, and the staff who purchase supplies, perform accounting work, and provide similar support.

Basic Departments of a Hotel:
酒店主要部门

■ **The Front Office**	前厅部
■ **Housekeeping Department**	客房部
■ **Food & Beverage Department**	餐饮部
■ **Business Center**	商务中心
■ **Recreation Department**	康乐部
■ **Engineering Department**	工程部
■ **Concierge**	礼宾部
■ **Human Resources**	人力资源部
■ **Security Department**	保安部

Hotel Types

Hotel Rating

Selection Tips

Scene One

Getting To Know Hotels

How to talk about hotels?

In this unit, you will:

- Practice talking about different types of hotels.
- Describe the features of hotels according to hotel ratings.
- Practice recommending the specific hotel to guests.

Brainstorm:

Have you ever stayed in a hotel before? Can you describe how it looked?

Warm Up

Look at the pictures of different hotels, and describe what type of hotel it looks like.

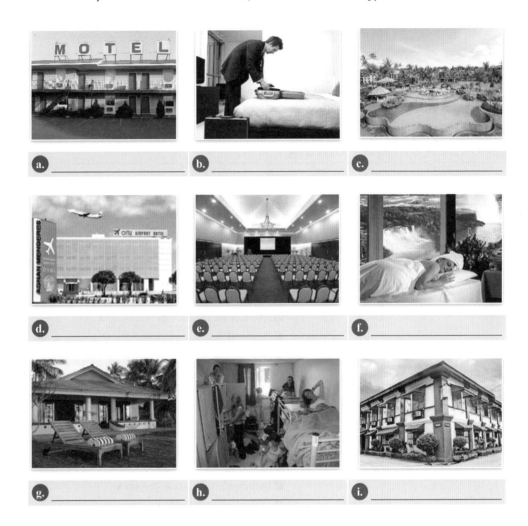

a. _____

b. _____

c. _____

d. _____

e. _____

f. _____

g. _____

h. _____

i. _____

Task 1: Hotel Types

Listen to the requirements from the guests and try to recommend a suitable hotel to them.

a. _____

b. _____

c. _____

d. _____

e. _____

f. _____

Useful Expressions

There are many kinds of hotels.

Different hotels **meet the needs of** different customers.

Our hotel **is considered to be** a Resort Hotel.

Practice:

Mention some examples in your neighborhood of the following different hotel types:
motel/resort hotel/airport hotel/health spa/holiday village/youth hotel/inn...?

Task 2: Hotel Rating

Please read the following information and try to understand the General Criteria of hotel rating.

Hotel Star	General Criteria
1-Star	■100 % of the rooms with shower/WC or bath tub/WC ■Daily room cleaning ■100 % of the rooms with color-TV ■Table and chair ■Soap or body wash ■Reception service ■Breakfast
2-Star	■Breakfast buffet ■Reading light next to the bed ■Bath or shower gel ■Bath towels ■Toothbrush, toothpaste, shaving kit
3-Star	■14 hours Reception, 24-hour phone ■Bilingual staff ■Luggage service ■Beverages offered in the room ■Telephone in the room ■Internet access in the room or in the public area ■Hair-dryer, dressing mirror, luggage place ■Shoe polish utensils, laundry and ironing service
4-Star	■Lobby with seats and beverage service ■Breakfast buffet or breakfast menu card via room service ■Minibar or 24-hour beverages via room service ■Arm chair/sofa with side table ■Bath robe and slippers ■Cosmetic products (e.g. shower cap, nail file, etc.) ■Mirror, tray of a large scale in the bathroom ■Internet access ■Restaurant with more choices

续表

Hotel Star	General Criteria
5-Star	■24 hours Reception ■Multilingual staff ■Doorman-service or parking service ■Bellman service ■Spacious reception hall ■Personalized greeting for each guest with a present in the room ■Minibar and 24-hour room service ■Ironing service (return within 1 h) ■Shoe polish service

Useful Expressions

Our hotel is a **five-star hotel**.

There is a 24-hour room service in our hotel.

There are many restaurants in our hotel, **such as** a Chinese restaurant, a Western restaurant, and a Japanese restaurant.

Practice:

Read the above materials very carefully and try to discuss what are the specific areas focused on for the requirements of star categories?

Task 3: Selection Tips

Listen to the interview between a reporter and the manager of the Grand Hotel, and then answer the questions below.

a. How big is the hotel?

b. What about other facilities?

c. How about the location of the hotel?

d. What does the hotel offer to attract the foreign visitor specifically?

e. What about the famous Health Spa Center?

f. Does the hotel have much going on in the evenings?

Useful Expressions

What kind of hotel were you considering?

I think this one would **suit** you.

I hope you **enjoy your stay**.

The hotel **enjoys great views** overlooking the lake.

It's very **quiet** and **pleasant**.

We offer dancing, floor shows and a nightclub.

Practice:

Please look at these pictures and read the information of each hotel. Then discuss with your partner and answer the following questions:

• Which hotel is the newest one?

• Which hotel is the most convenient if you want to go the park?

• Which hotel is the most convenient for you to go shopping?

• Which hotel is suitable for a temporary night so that you can take a plane early the next morning?

• Which hotel is the most convenient for you to enjoy the local food?

• Which hotel is suitable for a business trip?

Hotel A

built in 2002	located in downtown
480 rooms	2 blocks from Shopping Center
3 restaurants	$ 280 ~ 650 per night
free parking	

Hotel B

built in 1989	walking distance to natural park
150 rooms	easy access to restaurants
2 restaurants	$ 150 ~ 198 per night
free Wi-Fi	

Hotel C

built in 1995	3 miles from the airport
280 rooms	shuttle bus to downtown
1 restaurant	free Wi-Fi
free laptop	$ 180 ~ 388 per night

Vocabulary

airport	['eəpɔ:t]	*n.*	机场
commercial	[kə'mɜːʃl]	*adj.*	商业的
congress	['kɒŋgres]	*n.*	国会；代表大会
convenient	[kən'vi:niənt]	*adj.*	方便的，实用的
downtown	[ˌdaʊn'taʊn]	*n.*	市中心，商业区
facility	[fə'sɪləti]	*n.*	设备
health	[helθ]	*n.*	健康
hostel	['hɒstl]	*n.*	旅社，招待所
inn	[ɪn]	*n.*	小旅馆
motel	[məʊ'tel]	*n.*	汽车旅馆
nightclub	['naɪtklʌb]	*n.*	夜吧，夜总会
overlook	[ˌəʊvə'lʊk]	*v.*	远眺，瞭望
resort	[rɪ'zɔ:t]	*n.*	度假胜地
spa	[spɑ:]	*n.*	休闲中心，理疗中心
youth	[ju:θ]	*n.*	青年，少年
access to			接近，使用
a home away from home			家外之家
5-Star / Five-Star			五星级（酒店）
room service			房内用餐服务
24-hour			24 小时营业
shuttle bus			班车
swimming pool			游泳池

Exercise

I. Please translate the following sentences:

1. 不同的酒店满足不同客人的需求。
2. 我们酒店是一家度假型酒店。
3. 我们酒店是一家五星级酒店。
4. 我们酒店提供 24 小时的房内送餐服务。
5. 您想住什么样的酒店？
6. 我觉得这家酒店适合您。
7. 酒店可以俯瞰湖面的美景。
8. 我们酒店有舞蹈、现场表演及夜总会。

II. Discuss with your classmates and decide what type of hotel would you recommend to the following persons?

Mr. Green: I am a business man. I will have 3-day business trip in Shanghai.

John Smith: I will go hiking with four friends. Are there any cheap places we can stay overnight?

Mr. Lee: I'm flying from London to Beijing in the late evening and continue to fly to Shenzhen early in the morning.

Mr., Mrs. Williams and 2 children: We are going to have a 5-day holiday in Hangzhou, China. We want to relax ourselves and enjoy leisure time with families together.

Mrs. Nicole: I am arranging the Annual Conference of our international company this week.

III. Try to write the exact name of each hotel according to the Logo given below.

 _____ _____ _____

 _____ _____ _____

 _____ _____ _____

 _____ _____ _____

m. _____   n. _____   o. _____

There are some useful informations to help you:

Top 10 Hotel in the world

No. 1 Inter-Continental (酒店集团)
▶ Inter-Continental (洲际酒店集团)
▶ Holiday Inn (假日酒店集团)
▶ Grand Metropolitan (大都会)

No. 2 NYSE：CD (胜腾集团)
▶ Super 8 (速8)
▶ Days Inn (戴斯)
▶ Ramada (华美达)
▶ Howard Johnson (豪生)

No. 3 Marriott (万豪国际集团)
▶ Ritz-Carlton (丽思·卡尔顿)
▶ JW.Marriott (JW万豪)
▶ Marriott (万豪)
▶ Renainsance (万丽)

No. 4 ACCOR (雅高)
▶ Sofitel (索菲特)
▶ Novotel (诺富特)
▶ Ibis (宜必思)

No. 5 Hilton International (希尔顿国际)
▶ Hilton Hotel (希尔顿)
▶ Conrad Hotel (港丽)
▶ Scandic (斯堪的克)
▶ Double Tree (双树)
▶ Embassy Suites (大使套房酒店)

▶ Homewood Suites (家木套房酒店)
▶ Harrison Conference Center (哈里逊会议中心)
▶ Garden Inn (庭园旅馆)
▶ Hampton Inn Suites (汉普顿旅馆)
▶ Hilton Grand Vacations Clubs (希尔顿度假俱乐部)

No. 6 Choice Hotels International (精选国际酒店)

No. 7 Best Western International，Inc. (最佳西方国际集团)

No. 8 Starwood Hotels & Resorts Worldwide (喜达屋国际酒店集团)
▶ St.Regis (瑞吉斯)
▶ The luxury Collection (至尊精选)
▶ Sheraton (喜来登)
▶ Westin (威斯汀)
▶ FourPoints (福朋)
▶ W Hotels (W 酒店)
▶ Le MERIDIEN (美丽殿)

No. 9 Carlson Hotels Worldwide (卡尔森酒店集团)
▶ Regent Hotels & Resorts (丽晶)
▶ Radisson (丽笙)
▶ Park Plaza （丽亭）

No. 10 Hyatt Hotels / Hyatt International (凯悦集团)
▶ Hyatt Regency (凯悦)
▶ Grand Hyatt (君悦)
▶ Park Hyatt (柏悦)
▶ Andaz (安达仕)

Part 2

The Front Desk
前厅服务英语

Front Desk Introduction
前厅部简介

The Front Desk is the answer station for residence halls. If you have any questions about housing, or need assistance from Housing staff, or directions to a new location, stop by or call and ask the desk staff. They are all knowledgeable about the hotel, the nearby places, and the city. In most hotels, the Front Desk is located near the main entrance. Also, you register, check-in, check-out, change money and ask for other helps there, so the Front Desk is an open window of a hotel.

Main Functions of the Front Desk
前厅部主要功能

- **Room Reservation Service**　　客房预订服务
- **Check-in Service**　　入住登记服务
- **Concierge Service**　　礼宾服务
- **Information Inquiry Service**　　信息问询服务
- **Business Center**　　商务中心
- **Check-out Service**　　离店结账服务

| Room Type | Room Rate | Receiving Room Reservations |

Scene One | Room Reservations

How to make a reservation?

In this unit, you will:

- Practice talking about room types in a hotel.
- Describe the room rates of hotels.
- Practice receiving room reservations.

Brainstorm:

How many types of table reservations do you know?

Warm Up

Look at the pictures of different rooms in the hotel. Please discuss their differences and write down the possible room types.

a. _____

b. _____

c. _____

d. _____

e. _____

f. _____

g. _____

h. _____

i. _____

j. _____

k. _____

l. _____

Task 1: Room Type

Please book the suitable rooms for the persons mentioned.

1. Mr. and Mrs. Green: _____

2. Ms. Lim: _____

3. Miss Chen and Mrs. Lee: _____

4. Mr. Brown's company (a party of six, all men): _____

5. A family of three: Mr. James, Mrs. James and their 7-year-old son: _____

Useful Expressions

We have single rooms, double rooms **and** suites.

A single room means a room assigned to one person ...

A Queen room means a room with a queen sized bed ...

Practice:

What type of customers would usually book a **single room/twin room/suite ...** ?

Task 2: Room Rate

TARIFF/Room Rate - the rate charged daily for a hotel room.

Room Type	Number of People in Room	Per Night Rate*
Suite	1 or 2	$469.00
Deluxe Room	1 or 2	$424.00
Premium Room	1 or 2	$344.00
Premium Room	3	$388.00
Premium Room	4	$433.00
Standard Room	1 or 2	$317.00
Standard Room	3	$362.00
Standard Room	4	$406.00
Inside Room (no window)	1 or 2	$268.00
Inside Room (no window)	3	$313.00
Inside Room (no window)	4	$357.00

Useful Expressions

It's RMB 150 yuan / 388 dollars **per night**.

How many nights, please?

How long will you be staying?

We have 342 rooms **in all**.

The rate includes three full meals/breakfast.

It has twin beds.

Practice:

In pairs, ask and answer the following questions based on the tariff list given. Please answer with complete sentences.

a. How much do you charge for a Standard Room/Deluxe Room...?

b. Can I have a Standard Room as a single and how much do you charge for that?

c. Is breakfast included in the room rates?

d. What does an "Inside Room" mean?

e. How much do you charge for the cheapest room for two?

Task 3: Receiving Room Reservations

Listen to the dialogue and fill in the reservation list.

Lake City Hotel	
Guest detail	
Name _____	
Phone _____	
Enter details	
Arrival date _____ (D/M/Y)	No. of nights _____
Departure date _____ (D/M/Y)	No. adults _____
Room number 613	No. children _____
Description	
▶ single room	
▶ double room	
▶ suite	
Tariff code <u>STANDARD</u>	
Room rate RMB _____ /night	

Listen to the dialogue again and write down the necessary information.

Staff:　Lake City Hotel, good morning. _____?

Guest:　Good morning. I'd like to book a room.

Staff:　_____? We have single rooms, double rooms, and suites.

Guest:　I'd like to book _____, _____. How much do you charge for a single room?

Staff: _____. And this weekend we have the discount so it will be 368 RMB.

Guest: Wow, that is great!

Staff: For _____, sir?

Guest: two nights.

Staff: May I _____, sir?

Guest: Tom Green. T-O-M, Tom. G-R-E-E-N, Green.

Staff: And your _____?

Guest: 206-605-0563.

Staff: Great. _____, sir. Tom Green, booked a single room for August the 4th. For two nights. And your phone number is 206-605-0563. Is that correct, sir?

Guest: Good. That's all settled then?

Staff: Yes, sir. And we _____. Goodbye!

Guest: Bye!

Useful Expressions

What kind of room would you like, sir?

We have single rooms, double rooms **and** suites.

May I know your name, please?

And your telephone number?

This weekend we **have a discount**.

Let me **confirm the details** with you, sir.

We **look forward to** seeing you next Friday.

Practice:

Discuss with your partner and talk about how to make a reservation.

Vocabulary

arrival	[əˈraɪvl]	n.	到达，抵达
available	[əˈveɪləbl]	adj.	可用的；可提供的（房间等）
departure	[dɪˈpɑːtʃə(r)]	n.	离开，启程
duplex	[ˈdjuːpleks]	n.	占两层楼的房间，复式房间
reserve	[rɪˈzɜːv]	v.	预订
reservation	[ˌrezəˈveɪʃn]	n.	预订，保留
studio	[ˈstjuːdiəʊ]	n.	小型公寓式套间
suite	[swiːt]	n.	套房
tariff	[ˈtærɪf]	n.	价格表

triple	['trɪpəl]	*adj.*	三倍的，三个的
adjoining rooms			相邻房
connecting rooms			连通房
king size			特大号
non-smoking room			无烟房
queen size			大号
room rate			房价

Exercises

I. Translate the following sentences:

1. 早上好，请问有什么需要帮助的吗？
2. 您想要什么类型的房间，先生？
3. 我们有单人间、双人间及套房。
4. 原本单人间每晚 488 元人民币。但是这周末我们酒店房价有折扣，价格为 368 元人民币。
5. 请问您住几晚？
6. 能告诉我您的姓名吗？
7. 请问您的电话是多少？
8. 让我跟您确认一下详细信息。

II. Discuss the following ways of making a reservation in a hotel and try to decide which way is your favorite and why.

By cell phone, online, face to face, by telephone, via fax, by writing letter...

III. Traveling the Web: You are going to make a reservation on the computer now. Work with your partner and make a reservation according to the information online.

Who, where, when, how many..., how long..., ...

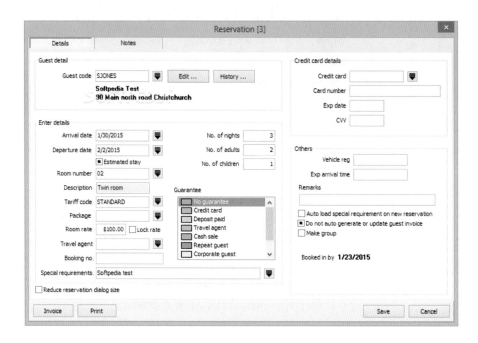

Tips

With the development of technology, some hotels in China now are loaded with artificial intelligence (AI) and robots, automating a series of procedures like check-in, lights control and room service. Guests can take the elevator or go to the restaurant and fitness center without any room cards, just "scanning face". "Turn on the lights, pull the curtains, turn on the TV..." Guests only need to speak to complete these tasks through voice control digital assistant. In the restaurant, it is also the robot waiter who serves the dishes to the guests. In the performance bar in the lobby, robot bartenders can make a variety of different wines and coffees.The AI-based solution can help customers save time and relieve hotel employees from repetitive work.

Receiving Guests

Introducing Services

Luggage Delivery

Scene Two   Bellman Service

How to provide bell service?

In this unit, you will:

- Understand the duties of the bellman.
- Master the useful expressions used in bellman services.
- Practice receiving guests and delivering the luggage to guests' room.

Brainstorm:

Do you know why the name "bellman?"

Warm Up

Look at the pictures of bell service in the hotel. Please discuss what the following things are and write down the possible words.

a. _____

b. _____

c. _____

d. _____

e. _____

f. _____

g. _____

h. _____

i. _____

j. _____

k. _____

l. _____

Task 1: Receiving Guests

Listen to the dialogues and try to finish the table below.

	The Number of Baggages (How many ...)	Details (What are ...)
Guest 1		
Guest 2		
Guest 3		

Useful Expressions

How many pieces of luggage do you have, sir/madam?

May I help you with your luggage, madam?

Let me **help** you **with** your baggage.

Are these **all your luggage**, madam?

Just a moment, please ... I'll **get** a luggage cart.

I'll **show** you **to** the front desk.

This way to the Front Desk, please.

By the way, the Front desk is **over there**.

Practice:

Work in pairs. One student plays the role of a bellman and the other is a guest. The bellman meets a guest at the hotel entrance, helps guest with his/her luggage and shows the way to the Reception Desk. Try to use the words and sentences in Part 1 and part 2.

Task 2: Introducing Services

Listen to the conversation and answer the following questions.

a. What's the room number of Mr. Drops?

b. Which floor is his room?

c. What are the services provided by the hotel?

　1st floor: _____

　2nd floor: _____

　3rd floor: _____

Useful Expressions

Your **room number**, please?

I will **show** you **to** your room.

This way, please.

Your room is **on** the 13th floor.

There is a Chinese restaurant, a western restaurant, a Japanese restaurant and a coffee bar **on the second floor**.

Practice:

Now please discuss with your classmates and talk about why the bellman need to introduce the service to the guest.

Task 3: Luggage Delivery

Now you will listen to a dialogue between a bellman and a guest. Try to fill in the following information.

Bellman: Here we are. This is your room. _____, please?

Guest: Here you are.

Bellman: May I _____?

Guest: Sure, just put them here.

Bellman: Ok. Here is the _____ in our hotel. We also have 24-hour room service. Shall I _____ for you now?

Guest: Yes. Thank you. Where's the price list for the mini-bar?

Bellman: It's in the_____. Is there anything else I can do for you?

Guest: No, thanks.

Bellman: You're welcome. I hope you have a pleasant stay here.

Useful Expressions

May I **have** your room card, please?

May I **put** your suitcase **on** this rack?

Here is the directory of services in our hotel.

Shall I **turn on** the air conditioner for you now?

Is there **anything else** I can do for you?

Practice:

Now please discuss with your partner and talk about the service procedure of a bellman.

Vocabulary

air-conditioner	['eərkəndɪʃənər]	*n.*	空调，空调机
backpack	['bækpæk]	*n.*	背包
baggage	['bægɪdʒ]	*n.*	行李
bellboy	['belbɔɪ]	*n.*	行李员
briefcase	['briːfkeɪs]	*n.*	公文包，手提箱
drawer	[drɔː(r)]	*n.*	抽屉
elevator	['elɪveɪtə(r)]	*n.*	电梯
luggage	['lʌgɪdʒ]	*n.*	行李，皮箱
suitcase	['suːtkeɪs]	*n.*	手提箱，衣箱
trunk	[trʌŋk]	*n.*	汽车后备箱
Beauty Salon			美容沙龙
bellhop / bellman			行李员（与 bellboy 同义）
Business Center			商务中心
coffee bar			咖啡吧
luggage cart			行李车
luggage rack			行李架
luggage tag			行李名牌
mini-bar			房内小冰箱
parking lot			停车场
travel bag			旅行袋，旅行包

Exercise

I. Translate the following sentences:

1. 我来帮您拿行李，好吗？
2. 先生，请问您一共有几件行李？
3. 请您稍等，我去拿下行李车。
4. 我会带您去前台。
5. 您的房间在 13 层。
6. 我可以把您的行李放在这个架子上吗？
7. 这是我们酒店的服务指南。
8. 酒店一楼有游泳池、美容院和咖啡吧。

II. Describe each item of the luggage.

leather , plastic, paper, Nylon, silk, ...

a white cotton bag   **a.** _____   **b.** _____

c. _____   **d.** _____   **e.** _____

III. Role-play:

Guest:

You're a businessman on a business trip. You arrive at the Hilton Hotel in downtown with a large suitcase and a piece of luggage in the morning.

Bellman:

You meet the guest at the front entrance of the hotel. You help the guest with his luggage, show him to the front desk and then show up to his room.

Tips

Talk about a bellman ...

A bellman, sometimes called a bellhop, typically works at a hotel or resort and reports to the bell captain. As one of the first employees guests encounter upon their arrival, it is important for this individual to represent the hotel in a professional, friendly manner. Greeting everyone with a smile, the uniformed worker may open doors, assist with luggage, and escort guests to their rooms. He often points out special features and amenities of the hotel. Someone in this position will generally do whatever he can to make guests feel at home during their stays.

When visitors first arrive at a hotel, the bellman will usually offer to take their luggage and packages. He delivers everything to the patron's room in a timely manner, via a large rolling cart. Many times, he will personally escort guests to their suites. Along the way, he may point out the gift shop, restaurants, swimming pool, weight room, or any other special features of the hotel.

Upon reaching the guest's room, the bellman may open the drapes or turn on lights. He may show guests how to access the mini bar or use the in-room safe. He will usually answer any questions a guest may have regarding check-out or offer directions to local area attractions. His job is to be gracious and hospitable.

Check-in With Reservation　　**Walk-in Guest Service**　　**No Rooms Available**

Scene Three　　　Check-in

How to check-in?

In this unit, you will:

- Learn how to make a registration.
- Master the useful expressions.
- Practice offering check-in service in different situations.

Brainstorm:

Do you have experience checking in a hotel?

Warm Up

Look at the pictures about the services of front desk. Please discuss what are the following things and write down the possible words.

a. _____

b. _____

c. _____

d. _____

e. _____

f. _____

g. _____

h. _____

i. _____

j. _____

k. _____

l. _____

Task 1: Check-in with Reservation

Listen to the dialogue and try to answer the questions.

a. What's the name of the guest? Can you spell it?

b. What kind of room did she book online?

c. How long will she stay in the hotel?

d. Which floor does she like? Why?

e. How does she pay for the room?

f. What's the room number of the guest?

Useful Expressions

Good morning/afternoon/evening, sir/madam.

Welcome to our hotel.

Can I help you? / **How may I** help you? / **What can I** do for you?

Could you **spell your name**, please?

May I **see your passport**, please?

Here is your room card. Your **room number** is 1386.

The elevator is **over there.**

Enjoy your stay.

Practice:

Please fill in this registration form with your own information. Then make up a dialogue with your partner on offering check-in service with a reservation. You and your partner will be the receptionist and the guest in turns.

Surname 姓	Name 名		Sex 性别	
Nationality 国籍	Place of Birth 籍贯		D.O.B. 出生日期	
Type of Visa 签证类别	Validity 有效期	Yr 年	Mth 月	Day 日
Type of Identification 证件类别	No. 号码			
Permanent Address 永久性住址 Home/Office 住宅/办公室				
Date of Arrival 到达日期	Date of Departure 离店日期		Room No. 房号	
Hosted by 接待单位	Purpose of Stay 停留事由: Travel 旅游　　Business 商务　　Official 官方活动			
Rate 房价	Method of Payment 付款方式: Cash 现金　　　　　　　　　Credit Card 信用卡 Traveler's Check 旅行支票　　Other 其他			
Remarks 备注				
A safe box Provided at Front Office or in the guest room is available for use free of charge 酒店前厅部及客房内的保险箱可免费使用				

Task 2: Walk-in Guest Service

Listen to the dialogue and try to fill the blanks.

Receptionist: Good morning, madam. _____. Can I help you?

Guest: Good morning. I'd like to check-in.

Receptionist: Do you _____?

Guest: No. I've just arrived in this city.

Receptionist: Please wait for a moment, madam. Let me see if _____. So what kind of room would you like, madam?

Guest: I'd like to have a single room with queen bed, if possible.

Receptionist: Yes, there is a single room with queen bed. _____, please?

Guest: Only one night. What's the room rate, please?

Receptionist: It's _____, including breakfast.

Guest: Very good.

Receptionist: May I see your passport, please?

Guest: Certainly. Here it is.

Receptionist: _____?

Guest: Ok. Can I pay by credit card here?

Receptionist: Sure.

Guest: Perfect. Here you are.

Receptionist: _____?

Guest: Certainly.

Receptionist: Thank you, madam. Here is your _____. Your room number is _____, on the sixth floor. The bellboy will show you up. Have a _____.

Guest: Great. Thank you!

Useful Expressions

Let me see if there is any rooms **available** now.

It's 459 yuan per night, **including** breakfast.

Would you please **fill the registration form**?

Could you **sign your name** here?

Here is your **room card** and your **breakfast coupon**.

Your **room number** is 623, on the sixth floor.

Have a **pleasant stay**.

Practice:

Now please discuss with your classmates and give the conclusion on serving steps of check-in service.

Task 3: No Rooms Available

Now you will listen to a dialogue between a receptionist and a guest. Decide whether the statements are True or False.

a. The guest wants to have single rooms. _____

b. The guest didn't have a reservation. _____

c. The hotel is very busy this week. _____

d. The guest wants to wait for rooms in this hotel._____

e. The guest wants to check in tomorrow. _____

Useful Expressions

How many people do you have, sir?

Sorry, we have **no vacant rooms** for you.

All the rooms are **booked up.**

But I can **recommend** you **to** another Hotel not far from here.

Practice:

Please fill in the blanks with proper English.

A: Good afternoon, sir._____(欢迎来到我们酒店). May I help you?

B: Yes, please. Do you have any double rooms available tonight?

A: _____(您有预订吗), sir?

B: No, I am afraid not.

A: _____(您一行几人)?

B: We are a party of four.

A: Just a moment, please. I have a check ... Sorry, we have no vacant rooms for you. Our hotel holds an international conference these days and _____(所有的房间都订完了) during this week. But I can _____ (推荐您去另外一家酒店). Maybe you can get vacant rooms there.

B: That sounds great. Thanks.

A: You are welcome.

Vocabulary

birth	[bɜ:θ]	*n.*	出生
brochure	['brəʊʃə(r)]	*n.*	小册子，手册
fill	[fɪl]	*v.*	填写，填满
lobby	['lɒbi]	*n.*	大厅
nationality	[ˌnæʃə'næləti]	*n.*	国籍
passport	['pɑ:spɔ:t]	*n.*	护照
receipt	[rɪ'si:t]	*n.*	收据
reception	[rɪ'sepʃn]	*n.*	接待
receptionist	[rɪ'sepʃənɪst]	*n.*	接待员
sign	[saɪn]	*v.*	签名
signature	['sɪgnətʃə(r)]	*n.*	签名，署名
book up			订光了，没有剩余的
breakfast coupon			早餐券
ID card			身份证
recommend to			推荐，建议
registration form			登记表
room card			房卡
room number			房间号码
vacant room			空房
waiting list			候房名单

Exercise

I. Please translate the following sentences:

1. 请您拼写一下名字好吗？

2. 请问我可以看下您的护照吗？

3. 这是您的房卡。您的房间号是 1386。

4. 您可以填写一下入住登记表吗？

5. 您可以在这里签名吗？

6. 这是您的房卡和早餐券。

7. 很抱歉，我们没有空房间给您了。所有的房间都订完了。

8. 但是我可以给您推荐另一家酒店，就在附近。

II. Please put the following sentences into the correct order to make the dialogue between a guest and a receptionist.

(　1　) Good morning. Welcome to our hotel. May I help you?

(　　　) Do you have a reservation, sir?

(　　) K-A-R-E-N. Karen.

(　　) Thank you. Karen, yes... so that's a double room with bath for 2 nights.

(　　) Yes, I reserved a double room a week ago.

(8) Yes, that's right.

(　　) Good morning. I'd like to check in, please.

(　　) Thank you, sir. Here is your key. It's on the sixth floor, room 638. Enjoy your stay.

(　　) Could you just sign here, please?

(　　) Could you spell your name, please?

(　　) Yes, here it is.

(12) Thank you.

 Role-play

Step 1:

> Student A:
> Write a list of 5 rooms which haven't been booked in your hotel for tonight. You need to make sure the room sizes and floors are different. Each room has an advantage and disadvantage.
>
> Student B:
> Write a list of 5 guests (singles couples, young /old age, male/female...) who want to have a room for tonight.

Step 2:

Please exchange your list of rooms with another group with the list of guests. Try to choose one of the guests and the rooms, then make up a dialogue between a receptionist and a guest on three conditions: check-in with a reservation, check in without a reservation, as well as no rooms available.

Tips

Skills of Check-in

No.1

Find out the guest's name immediately and use it at least three times during the conversation. Always use polite titles as "Mr." or "Ms." when addressing the guest. Do not call a guest by his or her first name.

No.2

Check the reservation in the computer and confirm the room information with the guest. If there is no reservation for the guest, you should check the reservation list for the vacancies and then introduce them to the guest.

No.3

Ask the guest to show his or her identification, such as ID card, passport or Officer's Certification. You can ask the guest in this way: "May I see some identification?" or "Could I see your passport?"

No.4

Fill out the registration form. On the form, fill in the guest's name (surname and first name), sex, the date of birth, the nationality, the valid card number, the detailed address, the dates of arrival and departure, and the room type and ask the guest to sign his/her name as well.

No.5

When handling the group check-in, confirm the group name and the number of rooms, and then ask whether there are any changes in the time schedule and the number of persons.

| Lost & Found | Giving Directions | Leaving a Message |

Scene Four

At Information Desk

How to provide information service?

In this unit, you will:

- Learn how to answer the questions of guests.
- Practice how to give directions to guests.
- Practice how to leave a message for guests.

Brainstorm:

What do you do when you lost items in a hotel?

Warm Up

Look at the pictures about the places and things. Please discuss the following things and write down the possible words.

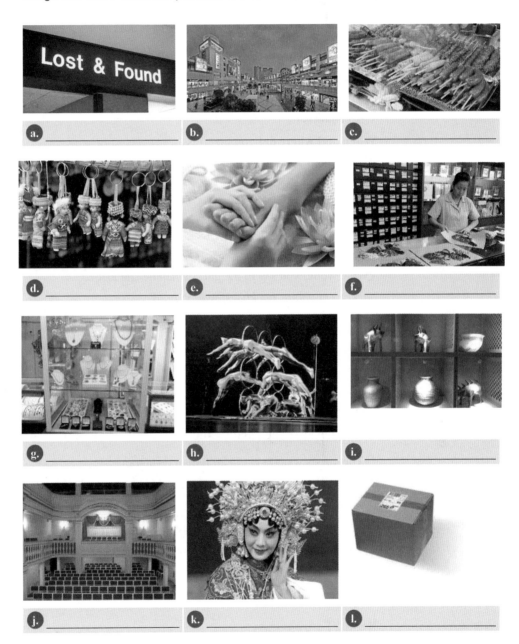

a. _____

b. _____

c. _____

d. _____

e. _____

f. _____

g. _____

h. _____

i. _____

j. _____

k. _____

l. _____

Task 1: Lost & Found

Listen to the dialogue and try to answer the questions.

a. What does the guest lose?

b. Could you describe the item? (make, shape, color ...)

c. When and where did the guest first miss it?

d. Where had the guest been this morning?

e. What's the guest's name and room number?

Useful Expressions

I'm **really sorry** to hear that.

Do you remember **the last time** you had it?

Could you give me **some information** about your watch?

What's the **make** of your watch?

What **color** is it?

When and where did you first miss it?

We will **help** you **find** it immediately.

Practice:

Please choose one of the following items and practice the dialogue with your partner by using the above sentences.

- What would you say to the guest when he/she lost ...

jacket, cellphone, backpack, wallet, book, ...

Task 2: Giving Directions

Now you will listen to a dialogue between a clerk working at the information desk and a guest. Decide whether the statements are True or False.

1. The guests want to eat in an Italian restaurant. _____

2. The clerk thinks the Dragon Boat restaurant is much cheaper and closer than the Red Palace restaurant. _____

3. The clerk suggests the guests to go there only by taxi. _____

4. The guests can take bus No. 320 and get down at Lake Station. _____

5. The clerk doesn't want to write the name of the restaurant in Chinese for the guests.

_____

Useful Expressions

The most famous one in the city is Red Palace restaurant **on** Nanda Street.

It's **cheaper and closer**.

I would **recommend** that.

I suggest you take a taxi.

You can also **take bus** No. 302 and **get down** at Lake Station.

Then, walk **ahead** about 20 meters, and you will find the restaurant.

Practice:

Now practice the following phrases and give directions to your guests.

a. 向左转 / 向右转

b. 一直向前走（不转弯）

c. 沿着这条路走

d. 对面 / 紧挨着 / 在前面 / 在后面/在里面 / 在外面

e. 十字路口 / 拐角

Task 3: Leaving a Message

Listen to the dialogue and try to fill in the following messages for the guest.

Message Form	
To :	Room No. :
Date: 08/14/2015	Time: 9:45 am
From:	Telephone No. :
Telephoned _____　　　Will Call Again _____　　　Please Call Him / Her _____	
Message:	

Useful Expressions

Would you like to **leave a message** for him?

Would you mind giving me your telephone number so that Mrs. Lee can call back **if necessary**?

Thank you for calling, madam.

We'll tell her **as soon as** she comes back.

Practice: Directions

Translate the following dialogue.

A: Good afternoon, sir. May I help you?

B: Yes, please. I tried to contact Mr. Smith in room 2609, but he was out.

A: _____(请问您要给他留言吗?)

B: Yes, please. My name is Ryan. Could you ask him to call me back as soon as he arrives at the hotel?

A: Certainly, sir. _____(能问一下您的电话号码吗?)

B: Yes. It's 50866689.

A: 50866689. Is that correct?

B: That's right.

A: Certainly, sir. I will repeat your message. The message is for _____ (2609房间的史密斯先生) from Ryan. Please call him back at 50866689 when you arrive at the hotel. Is that correct?

B: Yes. Thank you very much.

A: You are welcome. _____ (他一回来我就会告诉他). Have a nice day!

Vocabulary

acrobatics	[ˌækrə'bætɪks]	*n.*	杂技
downtown	[ˌdaʊn'taʊn]	*n.*	市中心，商业区
inside	[ˌɪn'saɪd]	*adj.*	里面的，内部的
opposite	['ɒpəzɪt]	*adj.*	对面的
outside	[ˌaʊt'saɪd]	*adj.*	外面的，在外面
message	['mesɪdʒ]	*n.*	消息，信息
minimum	['mɪnɪməm]	*adj.*	最小的，最低的
museum	[mju'ziːəm]	*n.*	博物馆
parcel	['pɑːsl]	*n.*	包裹
theater	['θɪətə]	*n.*	剧场，剧院
wallet	['wɒlɪt]	*n.*	钱包
arts and craft store			手工艺品商店
as soon as			一……就……
Beijing Opera			京剧
bus station			公交车站
Chinese massage			中式推拿
Chinese traditional medicine store			中药店
get down			下车
Lost and Found			失物招领
metro station			地铁站
pick... up			开车接（某人）
post office			邮局
shopping center			购物中心
snack street			小吃街
souvenir shop			纪念品商店
walk ahead			向前走

Exercise

I. Please translate the following sentences:

1. 很遗憾听到这件事。您还记得最后一次见到钱包是什么时候吗?
2. 请问您可以描述一下您的表吗?
3. 您的行李是什么牌子、什么颜色的?
4. 我们会尽快帮您寻找。
5. 我建议您打出租车。
6. 您可以乘坐 550 公交车在中心站 (Center Station) 下车,然后往前走大概 5 分钟,您就能看到超市了。
7. 请问您要给他留言吗?
8. 她一回来我们就告诉她。

II. Suppose you are working at the information desk of a five-star hotel. Please work with your partner: one of you ask the directions of the following places, and the other one tries to answer the questions.

turn left/right, go straight, walk ahead, cross, next to, opposite, in front of, at back of, ...

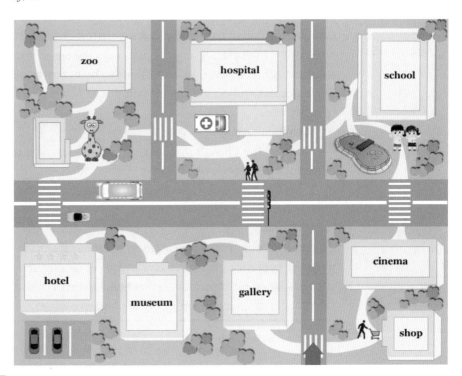

III. Discussion

What are the other services of the information desk in a hotel?

Skills & Qualities to Be a Desk Assistant

Customer Service

Desk assistants need to be as professional as possible, even in the face of complaints. They must have excellent customer service skills and be willing and able to assist people. Having the personal qualities of friendliness, motivation and a positive attitude helps desk assistants to be of better service. Desk assistants are most successful when they make their guests feel welcome and show a willingness to help them.

Communication

Communication skills involve speaking and listening to people. Desk assistants must respect visitors when communicating with them. They need to be reliable and have good listening skills without interrupting. And they must speak clearly and politely in the most effective manner.

Technical

Desk assistants must use a variety of technical skills to do their jobs. These skills might be operating phone systems, word processing and other software, printers, copy machines, fax machines and other equipment. Desk assistants must be able to take good notes, such as jotting down phone messages.

Payment Options

Bill Explanation

Express Check-out

Scene Five   Check-out

How to check guests out?

In this unit, you will:

● Learn how to check guests out.

● Master the useful expressions.

● Practice offering check-out service in different situations.

Brainstorm:

What is your best experience to check-out in a hotel?

Warm Up

Look at the pictures about the things you will see at the cashier's desk. Please discuss what are the following things and write down the possible words.

a. _____ b. _____ c. _____

d. _____ e. _____ f. _____

g. _____ h. _____ i. _____

j. _____ k. _____ l. _____

Task 1: Payment Options

Listen to the dialogue and try to answer the questions.

a. What is the name and the room number of the guest?

b. How much is the bill?

c. What is included in the bill?

d. Does the guest have a pleasant stay here in the hotel?

e. In which way does the guest pay for the room rate?

f. What kind of card does the guest have?

Useful Expressions:

How was your stay, Mr. Black?

Here is your bill. It's RMB 1384, **including** the 10% service charge.

How do you want to pay, sir?

In cash, with checks **or** by credit card?

What kind of card do you have?

Please take your credit card and **keep the invoice**.

I hope you **had a nice stay** here.

Practice:

Please discuss with your classmates and try to write down the advantages and disadvantages of following payment options.

Payment Options	Advantages	Disadvantages
cash		
traveler's checks		
credit cards		

Task 2: Bill Explanation

Listen to the dialogue and try to fill in the blanks.

Guest:　Good morning. I'd like to_____, please.

Cashier:　Good morning, madam. May I have your name and your room number, please?

Guest:　Mary Brown, _____.

Cashier:　All right. May I have the room card, please?

Guest:　Sure, here you are.

Cashier:　You checked in on the _____, is that right?

Guest: Yes.

Cashier: Fine, Ms. Brown. Here is your bill: three nights at _____ each, breakfasts on_____, and a phone call. Would you please go over the bill again and see if there is anything wrong?

Guest: Sure. ...By the way, what's this for?

Cashier: Well, this is the_____.

Guest: Oh, I see ... Thanks.

Cashier: So would you like to use the same _____ you gave us when you check in?

Guest: Yes, that's right.

Cashier: Would you like to sign your name here?

Guest: Sure. Here it is.

Cashier: Thank you. There you are, Ms. Brown. See you next time._____! Goodbye.

Guest: Thanks. Bye!

Useful Expressions

May I have the **room card**, please?

You checked in on the evening of October 5th, **is that right**?

Three nights at RMB 468 each, **breakfast** onWednesday and Thursday morning, and **a phone call**.

Would you please **go over the bill again** and see if there is anything wrong?

So would you like to use **the same credit card** you gave us when you check-in?

Have a **safe trip** home!

Practice:

Now please practice explaining the following bill to your guests. Try to make up a dialogue by using the sentences learnt above.

Nights Stay: 3	Room Rent per Night: 1180.00	Total Room Rent: 3540.00
		Bed Tax 10.00%: 354.00
		Breakfast: 128.00
		Bar Drinks: 150.00
		Parking fee: 240.00

Task 3: Express Check-out

Now please read the following bill of express check-out in Sunny Hotel and answer the following questions.

Date	Time	Description	Charges (USD)	Credits (USD)
11-JULY-2015	13:22	DEPOSITE		-195.30
11-JULY-2015	23:04	ROOM CHARGE	169.00	
11-JULY-2015	23:04	ROOM TAX	23.99	
12-JULY-2015	08:47	RESORT FEE	32.54	
		**Total	225.53	-195.30

***Balance   30.23

PAYMENT RECEIVED BY: VISA

Thank you for choosing Sunny Hotel! Express Check-Out allows you to check out of your hotel without having to return to the Front Desk. The credit card you used at check-in is billed for your charges or purchases during your stay, and this is the copy of your bill that appears under your door on the morning of your departure.

Questions:

a. How many nights does the guest stay in the hotel?

b. How much is the room rate?

c. How much deposit does the guest pay?

d. Will the guest pay extra money for the bill? How much?

e. Does the guest have to go back to the front office to check out?

f. How does the guest pay for the bill?

Useful Expressions:

You can **pay your deposit** using a credit card.

Express check-Out **allows** you to check-out **without** having to return to the Front Desk.

The credit card you used at check-in **is billed for** your charges during your stay.

This is the **copy** of your bill.

Practice:

Now please discuss with your classmates and give the conclusion on serving steps of check-out service.

Vocabulary

balance	[ˈbæləns]	*n.*	（账单）余额
bill	[bɪl]	*n.*	账单，清单；*v.* 给……开账单
cash	[kæʃ]	*n.*	现金
cashier	[kæˈʃɪə(r)]	*n.*	出纳员，结账员
check	[tʃek]	*n.*	支票；*v.* 检查，核对
deposit	[dɪˈpɒzɪt]	*n.*	押金，保证金
invoice	[ˈɪnvɔɪs]	*n.*	发票
tax	[tæks]	*n.*	税，税额
total	[ˈtəʊtl]	*adj.*	全部的，总的；*v.* 总计
American Express			美国运通卡
ATM: Automatic Teller Machine			自动取款机
check out			结账离店
credit card			信用卡（可以透支）
debit card			借记卡（无法透支）
MasterCard			万事达卡
POS machine: point of sale			刷卡机，销售终端机
resort fee			度假村费用
service charge			服务费
Visa			维萨卡

Exercise

I. Please translate the following sentences:

1. 一共是 2158 元人民币，包括 10% 的服务费。

2. 先生，请问您如何结账？现金、支票还是信用卡？

3. 请问您是哪种信用卡？

4. 请收好您的信用卡和发票，希望您在这里过得愉快。

5. 您是在 8 月 6 日晚上入住的，是吗？

6. 这是您的账单：588 元一晚、两个晚上，今早的早餐以及两份报纸。

7. 请您再浏览一下账单，看看有没有什么问题呢？

8. 您使用您登记入住的那张信用卡吗？

II. Please put the sentences into the right order. The first one has been done for you.

(1) Good morning. I'd like to check out now.

(　) Did you enjoy your stay, Ms. Grace?

(　) Here is your bill and please take a look to see if there is anything wrong.

(　) Of course, madam. What's your name and your room number, please?

(　) Thank you. Would you please sign your name here?

(   ) Yes, that's very correct. Can I pay by credit card?

(   ) I am Grace from room 263.

(   ) Master Card. Here you are.

(   ) Yes, it's very nice. Thank you.

(   ) Certainly. What kind of credit card do you have?

(   ) Ok. Here it is.

(   ) Thank you.Please take your card and keep the invoice. Have a nice trip!

 Role-play

Guest:

You are Robert Lee in room 2716. You are going to the front desk to check out. You only have the American Express card. You want to know if you can pay by the credit card.

Cashier:

You are working at the front desk. You are going to check the guest out. Robert Lee's bill is RMB1230, including service fee and 2 newspaper. American Express card is acceptable. Please present and explain the bill to the guest.

Tips

Do you know the express check-out at the Disney resort?

Express Check-out is available to all Disney resort guests staying in an on-site hotel, and paying for their room using a recognized credit card. When you first check into your room, if you're paying by Credit Card, an imprint will be taken at check-in, both for the full cost of your room, and also to allow you to charge purchases made in the parks back to your room, and hence back to your credit card. Express Check-out is a fast check-out method, that basically means that you don't need to go through the normal check-out process of visiting the hotel's front-desk, queueing for your bill to be made-up, and then checking your bill and paying for any additional expenses. During the last night of your stay, the front-desk will prepare your bill, and will tie it to the door-handle of your hotel room overnight. This bill will list the full amount that will be charged to the credit card imprint taken at check-in, and will include the cost of the room, along with any additional items that have been charged back to your room. If you've paid for a fully inclusive package through a travel agent before arriving, the express check-out bill will simply detail the purchases that you've charged back to the room. Providing the bill is right, you don't need to take any further action, and can simply load your vehicle and leave Disney property as soon as you're ready, without having to visit the front desk. You only need to do anything if the bill isn't right, or if you have any queries about it.

Housekeeping Department
客房服务英语

Housekeeping Department Introduction
客房部简介

The Housekeeping Department is one of the main operational departments of a hotel. Its duty is to ensure the cleanliness and good order of all rooms and public areas in the hotel, and provide all good and necessary services in order to create an ideal living environment. To keep the operation of the hotel going smoothly, it must also coordinate the work closely with other departments.

Main Functions of the Housekeeping Department
客房部主要功能

- **Chamber Service** 客房服务
- **Laundry Service** 洗衣服务
- **Room Service** 客房用餐服务
- **Turn-down Service** 做夜床服务
- **Special Services** 特殊服务
- **Maintenance Service** 维修服务
- **Miscellaneous Service** 其他服务

Guiding Guests to Their Rooms

Introducing the Room Facilities

Answering Questions

Scene One   Receiving Guests

How to receive guests?

In this unit, you will:

- Understand how to guide guests to their rooms.
- Practice introducing room facilities to guests.
- Practice answering guests' questions.

Brainstorm:

What are the duties of a floor attendant?

Warm Up

Look at the pictures of room facilities in the hotel. Please discuss about their names and write down the possible room facilities.

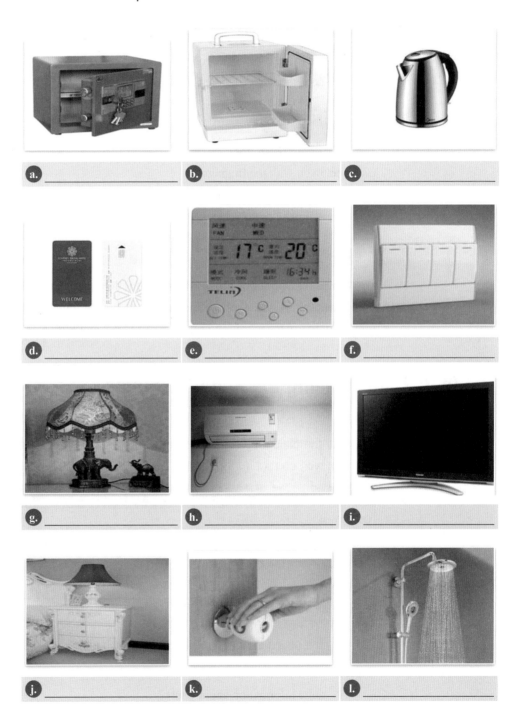

a. _____

b. _____

c. _____

d. _____

e. _____

f. _____

g. _____

h. _____

i. _____

j. _____

k. _____

l. _____

Task 1: Guiding Guests to Their Rooms

Listen to the dialogue and try to answer the questions.

a. What's the room number of the guest?

b. How does the floor attendant know the guest's room number?

c. Does the guest carry luggage with him?

d. How does the guest like the room?

e. Where does the floor attendant put the guest's suitcase?

Useful Expressions

Welcome to **the tenth floor**.

Can I help you with the **luggage**?

Can I show you to **your room**?

If you need any help, **do let us know**.

Practice:

Work in pairs. One student plays the role of a floor attendant and the other a guest. The floor attendant meets a guest , helps guest with his/her luggage and shows the way to the room. Try to use the words and sentences in Part 1 and Part 2.

Task 2: Introducing the Room Facilities

Listen to the dialogue, try to find what room facilities the guest can find and fill in the form with correct information.

Location	Room Facilities	Function
On the desk		
In the closet		
On the table		
Next to the door		
In the wardrobe		

Listen to the dialogue again and try to fill the blanks.

Guest: It's my first time to _____ at your hotel. Can you give me some information about your _____?

FA: Yes, all our hotel rooms _____ mini-bar, telephone, radio, TV, safe and _____. This is bedside panel and it can get remote control of lighting, TV, and signs for "make up room" and "_____".

Guest: Great. What's this on the desk?

FA: It's hotel manual. Hotel manual gives you information about our hotel, and _____.

Guest: Oh, I see. Then, what's this on the closet?

FA: It's a kettle for you to _____ in the room.

Guest: Thank you. What's this closet?

FA: There are mini-bar and safe in it. Some popular drinks and snacks are provided on a reasonable _____ in the mini-bar and you can _____ such as laptop and iPad in the safe.

Guest: Well, what's this next to the door?

FA: It's a _____ to hold your luggage to a comfortable height.

Guest: Um, I got it. Do you have trouser-press? I need to _____.

FA: Yes. It's in this wardrobe.

Guest: Good. By the way, can I get Wi-Fi in the room?

FA: Yes. Free Wi-Fi is _____ in all guest rooms.

Guest: Thank you very much.

FA: You are welcome.

Useful Expressions

Can you give me **some information about** your room facilities?

All our hotel rooms **are equipped with** mini-bar, telephone, radio and TV.

What's this on the desk?

Can I get Wi-Fi in the room?

Free Wi-Fi is **available** in all guest rooms.

You can **keep valuables** such as laptop and iPad in the safe.

Do you have an iron?

Practice:

Now please discuss with your classmates about how to introduce room facilities.

Task 3: Answering Questions

Now you will listen to a dialogue between a guest and a room attendant. Please put the sentences in order.

_____Put your valuables in and close the door.

_____Open the safe door.

_____Turn the dial quickly, and the safe is locked.

_____When "Open" is showed on the front of the door, inset the code by inputting a six-digit password.

_____Remember this number, you'll need it to open the door again.

Useful Expressions

Can you tell me **how to use** the safe?

Put your valuables **in**.

Please **remember** this number.

Set the code by inputting a **six-digit password**.

Then, put your valuables in and **close the door**.

Let me **have a try**.

Practice:

Please fill in the blanks with proper English.

G: Can you tell me _____(如何使用保险箱)?

O: My pleasure. First, open the safe door. When "Open" is showed on the front of the door, set the code by inputting a six-digit password. _____ (记住这个密码), you'll need it to open the door again. Then, _____ (放入贵重物品) and close the door. Finally, turn the dial quickly, and the safe is locked.

G: Oh, I see, _____(我来试试). Thank you very much.

O: You're welcome.

Vocabulary

closet	['klɒzɪt]	n.	壁橱
corridor	['kɔridɔ:]	n.	走廊，通道
code	[kəud]	n.	密码
cozy	['kəuzi]	adj.	舒适的
crease	[kri:s]	n.	皱褶，折缝，折痕
dial	['daiəl]	n.	钟（表）面，拨号盘
facility	[fə'siliti]	n.	设施
function	['fʌŋkʃən]	n.	功能
invisible	[in'vizəbl]	adj.	看不见的
manual	['mænjuəl]	n.	手册，指南
panel	['pænəl]	n.	控制板，面板
precede	[ˌpri'si:d]	v.	先于，处于……前面的位置
snack	[snæk]	n.	快餐，点心
spacious	['speiʃəs]	adj.	宽敞的

wardrobe	['wɔːdrəub]	n.	衣柜，衣橱
be equipped with			配备
Do Not Disturb			请勿打扰
floor attendant			楼层服务员
luggage rack			行李架
trouser-press			吊裤架

Exercise

I. Please translate the following sentences:

1. 我可以带您去房间吗？
2. 房间看起来很宽敞，床看起来很舒适。
3. 这是我们酒店的服务指南，它将告诉您有关我们酒店的服务及设施。
4. 您能告诉我一些房间设施的信息吗？
5. 我们所有的酒店房间都配有小冰箱、电话、收音机和电视。
6. 所有客房可以免费无线上网。
7. 您可以把贵重物品如笔记本电脑、iPad 放在保险柜。
8. 您能告诉我怎样使用保险箱吗？

II. Here is a dialogue about receiving guests. Please put the sentences in order to make the dialogue between the guest and the floor attendant.

_____ **A:** You are welcome.

_____ **G:** Yes. Can you show me my room?

_____ **A:** Ah, your room is 602. It faces the garden. It's lovely.

_____ **G:** Yes. Here you are.

_____ **A:** My pleasure. May I have a look at your room card?

_____ **G:** Wow, this is really what I want.

_____ **A:** Good evening, madam. Welcome to the 6th floor. What can I do for you?

_____ **G:** Thank you. It is very kind of you.

_____ **A:** This way, madam, please. Let me help you with your luggage.

III. Role-play

> **Guest:** You are Mr. Smith. You have just entered your room in the Grand Hotel. You want to know how to use the facilities in your room.
>
> **Room Attendant:** You greet the guest and make an introduction of the room facilities to him.

Hotel Meal Delivery Robot

Nowadays, various forms of intelligent devices are playing an increasingly important role in people's lives under the background of intelligent and connected life. Many hotels have meal delivery robots that can help deliver meals or items to guest rooms. While saving staff for the front desk, it has also become a highlight that children and even adults are very interested in. When we check in at the front desk, the staff will remind us to order takeout and write the room number directly. The takeout will be sent to the takeout service center at the front desk, and then they will help to send it to the room with a robot. When the robot gets to the elevator door, it doesn't need to press the elevator. It should be connected to the elevator system. The robot does not knock at the door. It will call the room and remind you in Chinese or English to open the door. Your meal has been delivered. It seems that different hotels have different settings. Robots in hotel bring us a lot of convenience.

Cleaning the Room

Asking for Extra Items

DND Service

Scene Two

Chamber Service

How to provide chamber service?

In this unit, you will:

- Describe basic steps for room cleaning.
- Practice asking for extra items.
- Understand how to use DND service.

Brainstorm:

Is housekeeping department important for a hotel? Why?

Warm Up

Look at the pictures of different items in the hotel. Please discuss about them and write down as many items as possible.

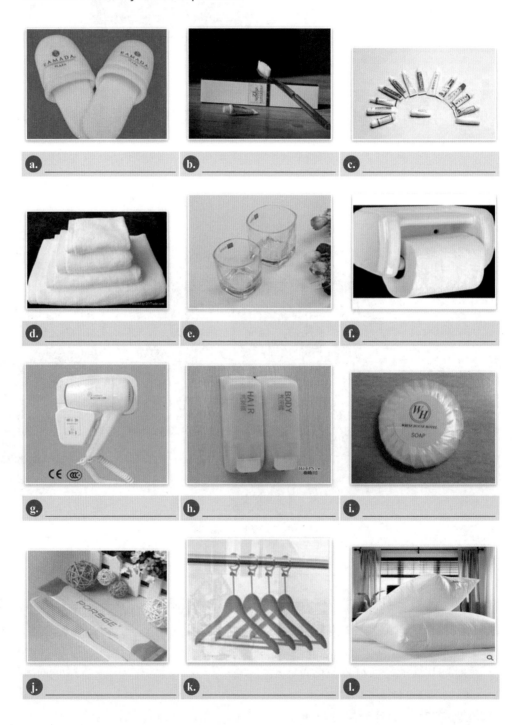

a. _____

b. _____

c. _____

d. _____

e. _____

f. _____

g. _____

h. _____

i. _____

j. _____

k. _____

l. _____

Task 1: Cleaning the Room

Listen to the dialogue and try to answer the questions.

a. What kind of room would the room attendant clean first?

b. Why should the check-out room be cleaned first?

c. When will the room attendant finish cleaning the room?

d. Why does the guest wish his room to be cleaned a bit earlier?

e. When will his friend come?

Useful Expressions

May I come in?

Would it **be convenient** now, sir?

Would you please come a bit earlier next time?

We usually have to clean the **check-out room** unless there is a request.

We'll try our best to provide a clean room **in half an hour**.

Practice:

Now please discuss with your classmates the sequence of cleaning the following types of rooms during the peak season.

VIP rooms

check-out room

rooms with "please clean it right away" sign

other guest rooms

Task 2: Asking for Extra Items (Adding Items)

Listen to the dialogue and try to fill the blanks.

Attendant: Housekeeping. What can I do for you?

Guest: Yes, could you please bring me a _____? I feel cold.

Attendant: OK, which room are you in?

Guest: 1018. Besides, can you _____ some more_____, please? My friends will come.

Attendant: No problem. Is there anything _____ you need, madam?

Guest: Yes. Would you please _____ me a sewing kit? I need to sew some buttons onto a shirt and I need some more _____.

Attendant: All right. I'll get someone to bring some up _____.

Guest: Thank you.

Attendant: You're welcome.

Useful Expressions

Could you please bring me a blanket?

Can you **send up some more** towels, please?

Is there anything **in particular** you need, madam?

I'll get someone to **bring some up a**t once.

We **need some more** coat hangers.

Would you please **bring me** a sewing kit?

I **need to** sew some buttons onto a shirt.

Practice:

Now please discuss with your classmates about how to ask for extra items in the hotel.

Task 3: DND Service

Now you will listen to a dialogue between a guest and a room attendant. Please put the sentences in order.

_____ It's DND button.

_____ It means "Do Not Disturb".

_____ What's this on the bedside panel, madam?

_____ If you need to rest in the room and won't be disturbed, you'd better turn on the "Do Not Disturb" sign.

_____ What does it mean?

Useful Expressions

It means "**Do Not Disturb**".

If you **need to rest** in the room and won't be disturbed, you'd better turn on the "Do Not Disturb" sign.

I want to have a good rest and **won't be disturbed**.

Please call me **whenever you need us**.

Practice:

Please fill in the blanks with proper English.

Guest: What's this on the bedside panel, madam?

Attendant: It's DND button.

Guest: What does it mean?

Attendant: It means "_____(请勿打扰)". If you need to rest in the room and won't be disturbed, you'd better _____(打开) the

"Do Not Disturb" sign.

Guest: Good. After a 7-hour flight journey, I want to _____(好好休息) and won't be disturbed. I'll turn the "DND" on.

Attendant: Wish you have a nice sleep.

Guest: Thank you very much.

Attendant: You're welcome. Please call me _____(如果有需要).

Vocabulary

ashtray	['æʃˌtreɪ]	n.	烟灰缸
blanket	['blæŋkit]	n.	毛毯，毯子
convenient	[kən'vi:njənt]	adj.	方便的
converter	[kən'vɜ:tə(r)]	n.	转换器，变压器
prepare	[pri'pɛə]	v.	准备
quilt	[kwilt]	n.	被子
recharge	[ˌri:'tʃɑ:dʒ]	v.	充电
robe	[rəub]	n.	睡袍，长袍
rug	[rʌg]	n.	小块地毯
sew	[səu]	v.	缝，做针线活
shaver	['ʃeɪvə(r)]	n.	剃具，刮刀，剃刀
tariff	['tærif]	n.	价格表
vacant	['veikənt]	adj.	空闲的，空缺的
voltage	['vəultidʒ]	n.	电压
check-out room			走客房
go ahead			表示同意
in particular			特别是
non-slip			防滑的；不滑的
peak season			旺季
sewing kit			针线包

Exercise

I. Please translate the following sentences:

1. 我们通常得先打扫走客房，除非客人提出要求。

2. 我们需要为另一个客人准备好空房间。

3. 您什么时候能够打扫完房间？

4. 您能给我拿条毯子吗？我觉得冷。

5. 我们需要更多的衣架。

6. 我马上找人送一些过去。

7. 如果您需要在房间休息，且不被打扰，您最好打开"请勿打扰"。

8. 七个小时的飞行旅程后，我想好好休息一下，不想被打扰。

II. Here is a dialogue about chamber service. Please put the sentences in order to make the dialogue between the guest and the floor attendant.

_____**A:** What time would you like me to come back?

_____**G:** An hour later.

_____**A:** May I clean your room now?

_____**G:** Yes. I'm out of toilet paper. Would you bring me more?

_____**A:** Housekeeping. May I come in?

_____**G:** Well, I'm a bit tired now. Can you come back later?

_____**A:** All right, I'll get it for you right away.

_____**G:** Come in, please.

_____**A:** Okay. Is there anything I can do for you before I leave?

III. Role-play

> **Guest:** Your 110V electric shaver is out of electricity and it needs recharging. But the voltage in the hotel is 220V. You need a converter. You come to the housekeeping department to borrow.
>
> **Floor Attendant:** Another guest has borrowed it. You promise to send it to his room in half an hour.

Tips

Background information

Status of the room:

OCC(Occupied)　　　　　住客房

VAC(Vacant Room)　　　空房

C/O(Check Out)　　　　　走客房

OOO(Out of Order)　　　待修房

Room Items:

BATH LINEN	Bath Towel, Hand Towel, Wash Cloth, Bath Robes
	Bath Rug, Non-slip Bath Mat, Laundry Bags
ROOM EQUIPMENT	Minibar, In-room Safe, Kettle, Television, Hair Dryer, Conditioner, High Speed of Wireless & Wired Internet Access
	Bedside Phone, Desk Phone, Bathroom Phone, Desk Lamp
	Glass Cup, Coffee Maker, Ashtray, Waste Paper Basket
	Bed Sheet, Bed Cover, Quilt, Pillow
ROOM SUPPLIES	Iron, Ironing Board, Hanger, Soap, Body Lotion, Shampoo, Shower Cap, Slipper, Toothbrush

| How to Get the Service | Filling in the Laundry List | Delivering the Wrong Laundry |

Scene Three
Laundry Service

How to provide laundry service?

In this unit, you will:

- Master useful expressions of laundry service introduction.
- Know how to fill the laundry list.
- Practice how to deal with the wrongly delivered laundry.

Brainstorm:

What kind of laundry service is provided in the hotel?

Warm Up

Look at the pictures related to laundry service. Please discuss about them and write down possible kinds of clothes.

a. _____

b. _____

c. _____

d. _____

e. _____

f. _____

g. _____

h. _____

i. _____

j. _____

k. _____

l. _____

Task 1: How to Get the Service

Listen to the dialogue and try to answer the questions.

a. When does the dialogue take place?

b. Why does Mr. Green call the housekeeping department?

c. Where is the laundry bag?

d. Will express service charge more than the same-day service?

e. Which laundry service does Mr. Green choose at last?

Useful Expressions

Can I **get the laundry service**?

If you have any, please **leave it in the laundry bag** behind the bathroom door.

How long does the laundry service **take**?

We **provide** same-day service, express service and next day service.

Express service only takes 4 hours with extra 50% charge.

Practice:

Work in pairs. One student plays the role of a laundryman and the other a guest. The laundryman answers the telephone and tries to introduce laundry service to the guest.

Task 2: Filling in the Laundry List

Listen to the dialogue and try to fill the blanks.

L: Housekeeping. May I come in?

G: Yes, please.

L: Good morning, sir. I'm here to _____.

G: Good. It's here.

L: Have you filled in the _____?

G: Yes. Here it is. I want the shirt _____ by hand in cold water and ironed, the suits _____ and ironed.

L: Well, sir, a shirt washed by hand in cold water and ironed, the suits dry-cleaned and ironed, 3 pieces _____?

G: Yes, that's right.

L: Which type of _____ will you choose? You didn't fill in the laundry list.

G: I'm sorry I forget it._____, please. Thank you very much.

L: It's my pleasure.

Useful Expressions

I'm here to **collect** your laundry.

Have you **filled** **in the laundry list**?

I want the shirt **washed by hand in cold water and ironed**.

Which type of **laundry service** will you choose?

Practice:

Please fill in this laundry list and make up a dialogue on offering the laundry service.

LAUNDRY SERVICE

Please complete this form and dial guest services extension. The total will be charged to your account.

Name:_____ Room No.:_____ Total pieces:_____

Date/Time:_____

Special Instruction

□ FOLDED   □ ON HANGER   □ REGULAR SERVICE   □ EXPRESS SERVICE

□ REGULAR SERVICE: Garments collected before 10:00 am will be returned the same day after 6:00 pm

□ EXPRESS SERVICE: Garments will be returned within 4 hours from the time of collection (latest collection 3:00 pm). A 50% Express Charge will be applicable.

DRY CLEANING

Guest Count	Hotel Count	Gentlemen	Unit Price (RMB)	Guest Count	Hotel Count	Ladies	Unit Price (RMB)
		Suit(3pes)	70.00			Suit(3pes)	70.00
		Suit(2pes)	60.00			Suit(2pes)	60.00
		Silk Shirt	35.00			Overcoat	50.00
		Trousers	30.00			Dress	30.00
		Sweater	40.00			Blouse	30.00
		Overcoat	50.00			Sweater	40.00
		Waistcoat	30.00			Pants	36.00

LAUNDRY

		Suit(3pes)	48.00			Suit(3pes)	48.00
		Suit(2pes)	40.00			Suit(2pes)	40.00
		Silk Shirt	20.00			Overcoat	20.00
		Trousers	15.00			Dress	15.00
		Sweater	20.00			Blouse	15.00
		Overcoat	20.00			Sweater	20.00
		Waistcoat	15.00			Pants	15.00

This form must be completed and signed by the guest. Guest's Signature	Sub Total
	Plus 50% Express Charge
	Plus 15% Surcharge
	Grand Total RMB

Task 3: Delivering the Wrong Laundry

Now you will listen to a dialogue between a housekeeper and a guest. Decide whether the statements are True or False.

1. The maid sent the wrong laundry to Mr. Green. (T/F)
2. Mr. Green's laundry is a white sweater and a black shirt. (T/F)
3. Mr. Green is in room 1018. (T/F)
4. The maid will bring the laundry to Mr. Green as soon as she finds it. (T/F)

Useful Expressions

The maid has just **delivered some laundry to** my room, but it's not mine at all.
We'll **check** it right away.
Could you please **describe your laundry**?
We'll **bring it up to** you as soon as we find it.

Practice:

Please fill in the blanks with proper English.

H: Housekeeping. May I help you?

G: Yes. The maid has just delivered some laundry to my room, but _____ (根本不是我的).

H: I'm sorry, sir. We'll check it _____(立刻). Would you mind telling me your room number, please?

G: Room 1018, Tom Green.

H: Mr. Green, could you please _____(描述) your laundry?

G: A black sweater and a white shirt, _____ (而不是) a white sweater and a black shirt.

H: We'll bring it up to you as soon as we find it.

G: I hope you can be more careful next time.

H: Thanks for your advice and we're very sorry for the _____(不便).

Vocabulary

attend	[ə'tend]	v.	参加
collect	[kə'lekt]	v.	收集
deliver	[dɪ'lɪvə(r)]	v.	传送，投递，递送
describe	[dɪ'skraɪb]	v.	描绘，形容
express	[ɪk'spres]	adj.	迅速的，特快的
extra	['ekstrə]	adj.	额外的

inconvenience	[ˌɪnkən'viːnɪəns]	*n.*	不便
iron	['aɪən]	*v.*	熨烫
laundry	['lɔːndri]	*n.*	洗衣房；洗好或待洗的衣服；洗熨
express service			快洗服务
fill in			填写
instead of			（用……）代替……，（是……）而不是……
laundry list			洗衣单
right away			立刻，马上

Exercise

I. Please translate the following sentences:

1. 如果有要洗的衣服，请把它放在浴室门后的洗衣袋中。
2. 我们提供当天服务、快洗服务和第二天服务。
3. 快洗服务只需要 4 个小时，但要额外收取 50% 的费用。
4. 我的这件衬衫要用冷水手洗，并熨烫。
5. 您填写洗衣单了吗？
6. 女服务员刚刚送了一些洗衣到我的房间，但不是我的。
7. 您能描述一下您的衣服吗？
8. 一旦我们找到，我们会尽快送给您。

II. Here is a dialogue about laundry service. Please put the sentences in order to make the dialogue between the guest and the laundry maid.

S=staff   G=guest

(1) Excuse me. Do you have any laundry? The laundry man is here to collect it.

(   ) That sounds reasonable.

(   ) Thank you.

(5) Please notify in the laundry list whether you need your clothes ironed, washed, dry-cleaned or mended and what time you want to get them back.

(   ) Don't worry, sir. The Laundry Department has wide experience in their work.

(   ) I see. What if there is any laundry damage? Does your hotel have a policy on dealing with it?

(   ) No, I have no laundry at present, thank you.

(   ) In such a case, the hotel should certainly pay for it according to our indemnity policy.

(   ) If you have any, please leave it in the laundry bag behind the bathroom door. The laundry man comes over to collect it every morning.

(   ) Not at all.

(10) All right. Thank you for your information.

Role-play

Guest:	You are invited to attend a party this evening. You tell the laundry maid that you want to have your dress washed in cold water and have the stain removed as soon as possible.
Laundry maid:	You explain the laundry service to the guest. As time is limited, you advise the guest to choose express service.

Tips

Symbols on clothes labels:

○	Dry clean	干洗
⊗	Do not dry clean	不可干洗
⊡	Iron	熨烫
⊡ ⊡ ⊡	Iron on low/medium/high heat	低温熨烫(100℃)/中温熨烫(150℃)/高温熨烫(200℃)
⊠	Do not iron	不可熨烫
△ ▲	Bleach/do not bleach	可漂白/不可漂白
□ ▥ ⊟	Dry/hang dry/dry flat	悬挂晾干/随洗随干/平放晾干
⊍	Line dry	洗涤
⊍ ⊍ ⊍	Wash with cold/warm/hot water	冷水/温水/热水机洗
✋	Hand wash only	只能手洗
⊠	Do not wash	不可洗涤
⊙	Tumble dry with low heat	低温转笼干燥
⊙	Tumble dry with medium heat	中温转笼干燥
⊙	Tumble dry with high heat	高温转笼干燥
⊠	Do not tumble dry	不可转笼干燥

笔记 | Notes

Part 4

Food & Beverage Department
餐饮服务英语

Food & Beverage Department Introduction
餐饮部简介

The Food and Beverage Department provides foods, drinks, and other relevant services for the guests. It's the representative department in the hotel management system because the working efficiency and service standard reflects the overall management of the hotel. Its service quality has great effects on the hotel's reputation and the selling of other products. The business involves in the western restaurant, the Chinese restaurant, the coffee shop and the bar, etc.

Main Functions of the Food & Beverage Department
餐饮部主要功能

■ **Chinese Restaurant Service**	中餐厅服务
■ **Western Restaurant Service**	西餐厅服务
■ **Banquet Service**	宴会服务
■ **Buffet Service**	自助餐服务

Receiving Reservations

Changing Reservations

Fully Booked

Scene One

Table Reservations

How to receive table reservations?

In this unit, you will:

- Understand how to receive table reservations.
- Practice how to confirm table reservations.
- Practice how to deal with the issues that fully booked.

Brainstorm:

How many types of table reservations do you know?

Warm Up

Look at the pictures about the services of table reservations in the restaurant. Please discuss and write down the possible words.

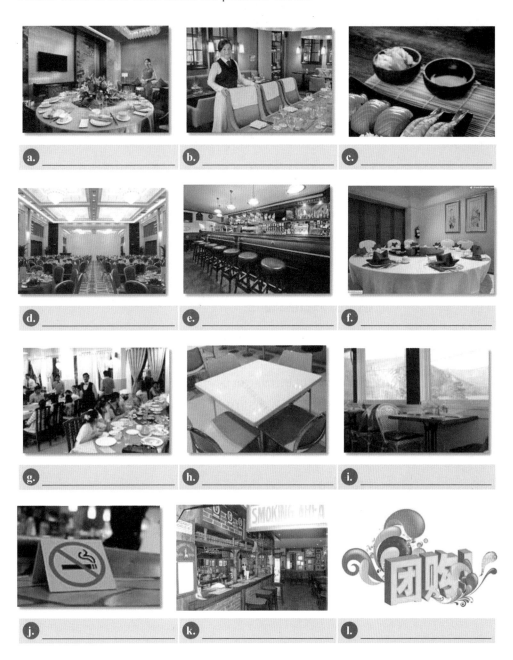

a. _____

b. _____

c. _____

d. _____

e. _____

f. _____

g. _____

h. _____

i. _____

j. _____

k. _____

l. _____

Task 1: Receiving Reservations

Listen to the dialogue and try to fill the following information.

Table No. 6		
Title	Mr. Miss Mrs.	
First Name		Last Name
Contact No.		
Status	RESERVED	
Person No.		
Arrival Time		
Note: (Special requirements, such as seats favorites, flavors, etc.)		

Useful Expressions

Good morning. Tulip restaurant. **How may I** help you?

For What time, please?

Would you like a table in the dinning hall or in a private room?

Your reservation **is confirmed for** tonight.

We look forward to seeing you.

Thank you for calling.

Practice

Please discuss with your partner and talk about how to make a table reservation in details?

Task 2: Changing Reservations

Now you will listen to a dialogue between a receptionist and a guest. Decide whether the statements are True or False.

1. The guest wants to reserve a table for six. _____

2. The guest postpones the dinner time until 8:30 p.m. _____

3. The restaurant only has two private rooms. _____

4. The restaurant cannot change the reservation for the guests. _____

5. The guest will come to the restaurant next Friday. _____

Useful Expressions

I'll **check** it **in** the computer.

Thanks for waiting.

Fortunately, we now have 3 private rooms, and one of them can **seat ten at most**.

Would you like to **take** it?

It's my **pleasure**.

Practice:

Now please discuss with your partner and answer the following question:

What are the main points usually changed by guests when they change the table reservation?

Task 3: Fully Booked

Listen to the dialogues and try to fill the blanks.

Staff: Good morning. This is Sally of the Grand hotel, Hawaii Restaurant speaking.

Guest: Good morning. I'd like to book_____ in your restaurant for our company group on _____.

Staff: Just a moment, please. I'll check our reservation list. Thanks for waiting. I'm afraid _____. You know it's very busy during the peak season. Would you like to make a reservation at another restaurant in the hotel?

Guest: Oh, what a pity! Where do you recommend?

Staff: _____?

Guest: Western food.

Staff: We also have Haiti Restaurant with _____ for up to 20 people. And it serves western food. Would you like to make a reservation in that restaurant?

Guest: That sounds great.

Staff: Ok. Could you _____, please? I'll connect you.

Useful Expressions

I'm afraid we are fully booked for that day.

Would you like to make a reservation **at another restaurant** in the hotel?

We **also** have Haiti Restaurant with large private rooms **for up to** 20 people.

Could you **hold the line**, please?

Practice:

Suppose you work in a restaurant of a hotel. Please discuss with your classmates and try to give at least three suggestions:

How can the restaurant maintain potential customers when it is full?

Vocabulary

banquet	['bæŋkwɪt]	n.	宴会，款待
bar	[bɑ:(r)]	n.	酒吧
confirm	[kən'fɜ:m]	v.	证实，确认
connect	[kə'nekt]	v.	连接，联系
fortunately	['fɔ:tʃənətli]	adj.	幸运地
instead	[ɪn'sted]	adv.	替代，而不是……
postpone	[pə'spəʊn]	v.	延期，延缓
private	['praɪvət]	adj.	私有的，私人的
season	['si:zn]	n.	季节，时期
a table for four			一张四人桌
banquet hall			宴会厅
Chinese / western / Japanese restaurant			中式 / 西式 / 日式餐厅
dinning hall			大堂
group-buying sites			团购网
hold the line			别挂断（电话）
instead of			代替……
private room			包间
smoking / non-smoking area			吸烟区 / 禁止吸烟区
window seat			靠窗的座位

Exercise

I. Please translate the following sentences:

1. 您订的餐位是想在大厅还是在包间呢？
2. 您今晚的预订已确认。
3. 感谢您的来电，期待着为您服务。
4. 太幸运了，我们只有 3 个包间了，其中一个最多可容纳 10 人。
5. 很抱歉，那一天我们已经订满了。
6. 您愿意在酒店的另一家餐厅订餐吗？
7. 我们还有一家餐厅可以提供容纳 20 人的大包间。
8. 您先不要挂断，我帮您接通。

II. Please speak out the following dates and times:

　　a. 9 月 12 日，2 月 6 日，8 月 17 日，12 月 3 日

　　b. 星期一，星期三，星期五，星期日

　　c. 上午 8:00，中午 11:30，下午 4:10，晚上 10:45

III. Role-play

A reservation staff is making a table reservation on the computer now. Work with your partner and make a reservation according to the information.

How may I help you? / For What time, please? / Would you like a table in the dinning hall or in a private room? / Your reservation is confirmed for tonight. We look forward to seeing you. /Thank you for calling. / ....

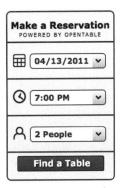

There are several useful sentences to help you.

Inquiring the Information:

How many people are there in your party?

When should we expect you, sir?

Under what name is this booking made, sir?

May I have your contact number, please?

Do you like the table in the hall or a private room?

Introducing the Restaurant:

We're open from 9:00 a.m. until 2:00 a.m.

Confirmation and Alteration:

Your reservation is for the Rose Room at 7:00 this evening. What else may I help you with?

When did you make the reservation?

We'll change the reservation for you.

Can Not Fulfill the Reservation:

I'm sorry. Our restaurant is fully booked at that time.

Sorry, we do not have reservation service today, because we have a banquet tonight.

Sorry, but there is only one table left that seats six people.

Receiving Guests

Seating Guests

No Seats Available

Scene Two — Greeting Guests

How to greet guests?

In this unit, you will:

- Master the useful expressions in greeting guests.
- Practice receiving and seating guests.
- Practice serving guests when no seats are available.

Brainstorm:

What's your experience of the best service in a restaurant?

Warm Up

Look at the pictures about the staff working in the food and beverage department. Please discuss and write down the possible words.

a. _____ b. _____ c. _____

d. _____ e. _____ f. _____

g. _____ h. _____ i. _____

j. _____ k. _____ l. _____

Task 1: Receiving Guests

There are many guests coming to Rose Palace Restaurant in your hotel today. Listen to the short dialogues and help the employee to make a record of the services.

Rose Palace Restaurant			
Dialogue 1	Reservation	Yes / No	
	No. of People	_____	
	Table position	Private Room /	Dining Hall
Dialogue 2	Reservation	Yes / No	
	No. of People	_____	
	Table position	Private Room /	Dining Hall
Dialogue 3	Reservation	Yes / No	
	No. of People	_____	
	Table position	Private Room /	Dining Hall

Useful Expressions

This way, please. / Please **follow** me.

Thank you for dining with us today.

Do you **have a reservation**?

Is this table all right?

How about that table near the window?

Shall I show you to your table now?

Practice:

Please discuss with your partner: "What are the service steps on greeting the guests?"

Task 2: Seating Guests

Now you will listen to two dialogues between a waiter and a guest. Then answer the following questions.

Dialogue 1:

1. How many guests will come to dinner?

2. What does the waiter say to recommend a table for them?

3. Are the guests satisfied with the seat suggested?

4. What does the waiter say when guests want to have the seat reserved by others?

Dialogue 2:

1. Is it easy to find a suitable table for the guest now?

2. Does the guest have the reservation?

3. What does the waiter say when they cannot seat the guest a table?

4. Does the guest agree to share the table with others?

Useful Expressions

How about the table in the corner?

I'm afraid that the table is reserved for 7:00p.m..

Sorry, I'm afraid we cannot seat you a table **at the moment**.

Would you mind sharing a table?

All right. **Come with me**, please.

Practice:

Now please discuss with your classmates the following pictures and try to use the following phrases to explain the table positions.

(in the corner, in the middle of, near the window, outside, in private room, in dining hall...)

a. _____

b. _____

c. _____

d. _____

e. _____

f. _____

Task 3: No Seats Available

Listen to the dialogues and try to fill the blanks.

Waiter: Good evening. Welcome to our restaurant.

Guest: Good evening. I'd like to_____.

Waiter: Do you have a reservation, sir?

Guest: No, we don't.

Waiter: _____, please. Sorry, sir, I'm afraid all the tables are taken and we have no seats available for you right now. Would you mind

_____ for a while?

Guest:　Oh, geez! How long will it take?

Waiter:　There will be a table for five in_____. You know that we are usually very busy during this peak season. Hope you can understand.

Guest:　Ok, that's fine. We don't want to change our dining location _____.

Waiter:　Certainly, sir. May I have your name please, sir?

Guest:　Richard Williams.

Waiter:　Thank you, Mr. Williams. If you don't mind, you and your friends can have _____ in the lobby first. I will inform you when we have the table soon.

Guest:　That sounds great. Thank you.

Waiter:　You are welcome. Hope you _____ in our restaurant.

Useful Expressions

I'm afraid all the tables are taken right now.

We have **no seats** available for you.

Would you **mind waiting** in the lobby for a while?

I will **inform** you when we have the table soon.

Practice:

Suppose you work in a restaurant of a hotel. What will you do if there are no seat available for your guests right now?

Vocabulary

afraid	[ə'freɪd]	adj.	恐怕的，担心的
bartender	['bɑ:tendə(r)]	n.	酒吧招待
busboy	['bʌsbɔɪ]	n.	餐馆工
captain	['kæptɪn]	n.	领班
chef	[ʃef]	n.	厨师，主厨
complementary	[ˌkɒmplɪ'mentri]	adj.	免费的，补充的
cook	[kʊk]	n.	厨师；v. 烹饪，做菜
helper	['helpə(r)]	n.	助手，帮手
hostess	['həʊstəs]	n.	（餐馆）女迎宾员
kitchen	['kɪtʃɪn]	n.	厨房
mind	[maɪnd]	v.	介意
palace	['pæləs]	n.	宫，华丽的场所
private	['praɪvət]	adj.	私有的，私密的
receive	[rɪ'si:v]	v.	接待，欢迎

seat	[si:t]	*n.*	座位；*v.* 使就座
server	['sɜ:və(r)]	*n.*	侍者，服务员，传菜员
share	[ʃeə(r)]	*v.*	分享，共有
steward	['stju:əd]	*n.*	服务员，管家
storekeeper	['stɔ:ki:pə(r)]	*n.*	仓库保管员，店主人
waiter	['weɪtə(r)]	*n.*	男服务员，侍者
waitress	['weɪtrəs]	*n.*	女服务员
weather	['weðə(r)]	*n.*	天气
enjoy the view of ...			欣赏……的景色
peak season			高峰期
wine steward			酒水服务人员

Exercise

I. Please translate the following sentences:

1. 拐角处的那个桌位可以吗？
2. 请稍等，先生。是的，我们有您的预订。我现在把您带到桌位吗？
3. 晚上好，先生。欢迎来到我们餐厅。请问有几个人？
4. 等会儿我们有桌位了就会通知您。
5. 那张桌位晚上 6:00 已经有人预订了。
6. 很抱歉，我们目前没有桌位安排给您。
7. 如果您不介意的话，您和您的朋友可以到大厅先喝些免费饮料。
8. 抱歉，我们目前没有空的桌位安排给您，您介意与别人合坐一张桌子吗？

II. Role-play: Please make up a dialogue according to the information below.

Student A:

Your name is Sophia. You want to invite 3 friends to have a lunch in the Summer Flower restaurant. You don't have reservation. You want to have a window seat if possible.

Student B:

You are working in the Summer Flower restaurant. It's very busy at noon and all the tables are taken. Try to explain to the guest and ask whether they want to wait or not.

III. Complete the dialogue below between the waiter and the guests.

Waiter: (欢迎客人)_____

Guest: Good evening. A table for five, please.

Waiter: (询问是否有预订)_____

Guest: No, we don't.

Waiter: (询问餐位是在大厅还是包间) _____

Guest: It will be fine in the dining hall.

Waiter: (询问靠窗的桌子是否合适)_____

Guest: Thanks! It's my favorite place in the restaurant.

Waiter: (请走这边)_____

Guest: Thank you.

Tips

How to create a quality atmosphere in a restaurant for guests?

When guests come to your restaurant, they should feel that they are in a special and comfortable place. Try these suggestions to create a home away from home for your guests.

Tip 1: Make deliberate choices with lighting. Consider your concept, and be sure the strength of the light suits the tone you wish to portray to your guests.

Tip 2: Choose music carefully. Make sure the volume of your music is audible but not distracting. Music should help create the ambience rather than overwhelm it.

Tip 3: Decorate appropriately. Decorate your restaurant with a special, unique theme.

Tip 4: Keep the restaurant spotless. Even a quick-service restaurant needs to demonstrate a high standard of cleanliness for customers to feel good about the quality of food.

Tip 5: Maintain the temperature. Maintain a comfortable inside temperature in your building. 20~21℃ is usually acceptable. Minimize drafts or hot spots from lights as much as possible.

Presenting Menus　　**Today's Special**　　**Making Recommendations**

Scene Three　　Taking Orders

How to take orders?

In this unit, you will:

- Practice how to present menus.
- Practice how to introduce today's specialties.
- Practice how to make recommendations.

Brainstorm:

Do you think taking orders is an important step in food and beverage service?

Warm Up

Look at the pictures about the items on the menu. Please discuss and write down the possible answers.

a. _____ b. _____ c. _____

d. _____ e. _____ f. _____

g. _____ h. _____ i. _____

j. _____ k. _____ l. _____

Task 1: Presenting Menus

A waitress is presenting a menu to a guest and taking the order now. Please listen to the dialogue and answer the following questions:

1. What should we say when we want to take orders for our guests?

2. Which one does the guest prefer, a la carte, fixed menu, or buffet?

3. What's his final decision?

4. Do you think the guest is satisfied?

Useful Expressions

Are you **ready to** order, sir?

It **comes with** fried rice.

You can have soup **instead of** salad.

This one is **preferable**.

I'll **make a note** of it.

Practice:

Please look at the following menu and work with your partner. Try to take an order and explain the content in turns.

Thanksgiving Day Simple Menu

Starters:

Sun Dried Tomato and Fetta Tarts*
Chicken and Rocket Sandwiches*

Main:

Roast Chicken (Nana to bring)
Roast Duck
Roast Beef
Leg of Ham (Poppy to bring)
Easy Potato Au Gratin*
Easy Pumpkin Au Gratin*
Honey Carrots
Steamed Greens

Dessert:

Granny's Christmas Pudding
White Chocolate Cheesecake*
Honeycomb Ice-cream Cake*

With Coffee:

Christmas Reindeer Biscuits*
Mini Christmas Puddings*

Task 2: Today's Special

Now you will listen to a dialogue between a waiter and a guest. Decide whether the statements are True or False.

1. On the special board today, they have roast turkey, vegetarian pasta and salmon sandwich. _____

2. The guest makes decision very quickly._____

3. The guest orders three dishes, including one special today._____

4. The guest wants the steak to be rare medium._____

5. The guest doesn't order any drinks._____

Useful Expressions

Please **take your time**.

I'll be back **in** a few minutes.

May I take your order **now**?

On the **special board** today we have roast salmon, vegetarian pasta and turkey sandwich.

How would you like your steak, sir? **Rare**, **medium** or **well done**?

What would you like **to drink**?

Let me **repeat** your order.

Practice:

Now please discuss with your classmates: "How to take orders?"

Task 3: Making Recommendations

Listen to the dialogues and try to fill the blanks.

Waitress: Excuse me, sir. _____?

Guest: Yes. We'd like to have some Chinese food. What would you recommend?

Waitress: We serve different styles of Chinese food here. Generally speaking, Cantonese food is_____, Sichuan food is_____, and Beijing food is a little bit_____.

Guest: We are not used to spicy food. Let me see ... do you have something special?

Waitress: If so, I suggest you_____. This stewed beef is stewed in red wine with_____. And this big portion is suitable for two of you.

Guest: Sounds great. We'll try that. Do you have any seafood?

Waitress: How about Shrimp Soup with Cream Corn? It's sweet and delicious. It's also very popular among our guests.

Guest: Yes, please.

Waitress: Any drinks?

Guest: _____, please.

Waitress: Certainly, sir. Just a moment, please.

Useful Expressions

What would you **recommend**?

We serve different styles of Chinese food here.

I suggest you **have a taste of** stewed beef.

This big portion is **suitable for** two of you.

How about Shrimp Soup with Cream Corn?

It's also very **popular** among our guests.

Practice:

Suppose you are recommending the dishes to your guests. Please describe the following pictures with the sentences learnt above.

(sweet, salty, delicious, hot, spicy, tasty, soft, light,heavy, popular, fresh ...)

Vocabulary

appetizer	['æpɪtaɪzə(r)]	n.	开胃品，开胃菜
buffet	['bʊfeɪ]	n.	自助餐
Cantonese	[ˌkæntə'niːz]	n.	广东人，广东话；adj. 广东人的，广东的
coke	[kəʊk]	n.	可乐（口语简称）
confirm	[kən'fɜːm]	v.	证实，确认
dessert	[dɪ'zɜːt]	n.	甜点，餐后甜食
drink	[drɪŋk]	n.	酒，饮料
entree	['ɒntreɪ]	n.	主菜
garlic	['gɑːlɪk]	n.	大蒜，蒜头
hot	[hɒt]	adj.	辣的，热的
light	[laɪt]	adj.	轻的，口味淡的
meat	[miːt]	n.	肉，肉类食物
medium	['miːdiəm]	adj.	中等的，半生熟的
menu	['menjuː]	n.	菜单
mushroom	['mʌʃrʊm]	n.	蘑菇
onion	['ʌnjən]	n.	洋葱

pasta	['pæstə]	n.	意大利面
portion	['pɔ:ʃn]	n.	一部分
potato	[pə'teɪtəʊ]	n.	土豆
rare	[reə(r)]	adj.	生的
recommend	[ˌrekə'mend]	v.	推荐
repeat	[rɪ'pi:t]	v.	重复，复述
salad	['sæləd]	n.	色拉
sandwich	['sænwɪtʃ]	n.	三明治
sausage	['sɒsɪdʒ]	n.	香肠
seafood	['si:fu:d]	n.	海鲜
shrimp	[ʃrɪmp]	n.	虾
soup	[su:p]	n.	汤，羹
stew	[stju:]	v.	炖，煨
strong	[strɒŋ]	adj.	强烈的，味道浓的
special	['speʃl]	adj.	特殊的，特色的
turkey	['tɜ:ki]	n.	火鸡
vegetable	['vedʒtəbl]	n.	蔬菜
vegetarian	[ˌvedʒə'teəriən]	n.	素食者
a la carte			零点菜肴，单点菜
beef steak			牛排
fried rice			炒饭
fixed menu			套餐
take order			点菜
well-done			全熟的

Exercise

I. Please translate the following sentences:

1. 请问您准备好点菜了吗？
2. 请您慢慢看，我几分钟后过来。
3. 今天的特色菜有牛排、鲜虾汤和火鸡三明治。
4. 您的牛排要几成熟？是三成熟、五成熟还是全熟？
5. 请问您想喝点什么？
6. 我们有各种样式的中国菜。
7. 这一大份正适合你们两人享用。
8. 奶油蘑菇汤怎么样？它在我们客人中很受欢迎。

II. Please give the recommendations to guests according to their needs.

Choices: *set meal, buffet, fast food, seafood, vegetarian food.*

1. A family wants to celebrate the birthday of the grandpa who loves fish. _____
2. A vegetarian who never eat meat. _____

3. Two businessmen want to have a standard meal with fixed price. _____

4. A party of five young people on traveling who want to eat quickly to save time.

_____

5. A company want to hold a conference in the restaurant. _____

 Role-play

Guest: You would like a club sandwich. You want to know if it comes with chips. Your second choice would be a small salad. You also like tomato juice. **Waiter / Waitress:** You take the order for this guest. Ask if he likes anything else with the sandwich. It's served with chips. Ask if he would like anything to drink.

Tips

Smart menu ordering system

Technology advancement has greatly influenced the business transactions. Business in catering industry has being improved with the help of digital systems such as the invention of smart menu ordering system.

In traditional ordering system, the customer has to wait for waiters to note down the order with pen and paper. It is entirely a manual process, low-efficiency and high-cost.

To overcome the limitations in manual system, smart menu ordering system is being developed to automate food ordering process. Smart ordering system is made more efficient and can help the manager to avoid human error and enhance business development as well as increasing the profit. In addition to high efficiency, the system is convenient, easy to use and can provide quality of service and customer satisfaction.

touch screen
ordering system　　　　Scan code order　　　　WeChat Mini
Program order

Describing Dishes

Offering Help

Asking For Opinions

Scene Four

Serving Dishes

How to serve dishes for guests?

In this unit, you will:

• Practice how to present menus.

• Practice how to introduce today's specialties.

• Practice how to make recommendations.

Brainstorm:

Why a waiter / waitress needs to be familiar with the menu?

Warm Up

Look at the pictures about the items used on the dining table. Please discuss and name them.

a. _____

b. _____

c. _____

d. _____

e. _____

f. _____

g. _____

h. _____

i. _____

j. _____

k. _____

l. _____

Task 1: Describing Dishes

Please listen to the dialogue and answer the following questions:

1. What does the waitress say to serve the dish?

2. What dish does the guest order?

3. What ingredients are in it?

4. Does the dish look good?

5. What part of chicken did the chef use in it?

Useful Expressions

May I **serve** the dish **now**?

Here is your food, *Sweet and Sour Chicken*. Please **enjoy** it.

We **cook** the chicken **with** black rice vinegar, eggs, soy sauce, and pepper.

It **looks** good, **smells** good and **tastes** good.

I hope all of you enjoy your food.

Practice:

Please look at these desserts and their ingredients. Ask and answer the questions in pairs:

A: *What's the ... ?*

B: *It's pastry filled with ... and ...*

Dish	Picture	Ingredients
Lemon Souffle		eggs, cream, lemon
Fresh Fruit Salad		different fruits in season
Trifle		fruit, cake, sherry, cream, custard
Tiramisu		eggs, biscuits, chocolate, marsala

Task 2: Offering Help

Listen to the dialogues and try to fill the blanks.

Waitress: Sorry to disturb you, sir. May I_____?

Guest: Sure. Go ahead.

Waitress: _____, please be careful.

Guest: Thank you.

Waitress: Would you like me to separate the soup for you?

Guest: Yes, please.

Waitress: Certainly, sir. ... well,_____, please enjoy!

Guest 1:   By the way, would you give me some more napkins, please?

Waitress: Certainly, sir._____.

Guest 2:   Also, I am not very good at using chopsticks. Can you bring me_____?

Waitress: No problem. I will be back soon.

Useful Expressions

May I **move** this dish to serve the soup?

This is **very hot**, please be careful.

Would you like me to **separate** the soup for you?

I will bring you **some more**.

I will be back **soon**.

Practice:

Please respond to the requests using *one, some, another* or *some more*.

Example:

A: Could I have some water? (get / some)

B: *Yes. I'll **get** (you) **some**.*

1. Can I have an apple juice, please? (get / one)

2. Could I have some bread? (get / some)

3. This spoon is dirty. (bring / another)

4. Our tea cup is empty. (get / some more)

5. My napkin is very wet. (get / another)

Task 3: Asking for Opinions

Now you will listen to two dialogues between a waitress and a guest. Decide whether the statements are True or False.

Dialogue 1:

1. The guest doesn't enjoy the meal at all._____

2. To the guest's opinion, the fish is too spicy._____

3. The guest orders Sichuan food._____

4. The waitress recommends Shanghai food to guest because it's very hot. _____

Dialogue 2:

1. The waitress asks the guest to pay the bill because it's nearly closing time. _____

2. The bill totals 484 yuan, excluding service charge._____

3. The guest wants to pay in cash._____

4. The guest has a visa card. _____

Useful Expressions

Do you enjoy your meal?

May I take your plate, sir?

How is the fish?

Just let me know if you need any help.

Do you need anything else?

Do you mind **if** I bring you the bill?

Practice:

Try to ask the guests' opinions using the sentences we have learnt today.

1. Ask the guest if he wants to see the desert menu.

2. Ask the guest about soup.

3. Ask the guest if he wants a coffee or a tea.

4. Ask the guest if you can take the plate.

Vocabulary

biscuits	['bɪskɪt]	n.	饼干
boneless	['bəʊnləs]	adj.	去骨的，无骨头的
bowl	[bəʊl]	n.	碗，碗状物
breast	[brest]	n.	胸脯

chocolate	['tʃɒklət]	n.	巧克力
chopstick	['tʃɒpstɪk]	n.	筷子
coaster	['kəʊstə(r)]	n.	杯托，杯垫
custard	['kʌstəd]	n.	蛋奶糊，乳蛋糕
fork	[fɔ:k]	n.	餐叉，叉子
glass	[glɑ:s]	n.	玻璃制品，玻璃杯
ingredient	[ɪn'gri:diənt]	n.	原料
knife	[naɪf]	n.	刀
Marsala	[mɑ:'sɑ:lə]	n.	（产于意大利西西里岛）马沙拉白葡萄酒
napkin	['næpkɪn]	n.	餐巾纸
pepper	['pepə(r)]	n.	胡椒，胡椒粉
placemat	['plesmɛt]	n.	餐具垫
plate	[pleɪt]	n.	盘子
skinless	[s'kɪnles]	adj.	无皮的，去皮的
separate	['seprət]	v.	分开，分离
sour	['saʊə(r)]	adj.	酸味的，酸的
spicy	['spaɪsi]	adj.	辛辣的，香的
spoon	[spu:n]	n.	匙子，匙
sweet	[swi:t]	adj.	甜的
tablecloth	['teɪblklɒθ]	n.	桌布，台布
taste	[teɪst]	n.	滋味，风味；v.品尝
tasty	['teɪsti]	adj.	美味的，可口的
teapot	['ti:pɒt]	n.	茶壶
tray	[treɪ]	n.	托盘
vinegar	['vɪnɪgə(r)]	n.	醋
soy sauce			酱油

Exercise

I. Please translate the following sentences:

1. 现在可以上菜了吗?
2. 这道菜色香味俱全。
3. 希望您们用餐愉快。
4. 我可以挪下这盘菜以便上汤吗?
5. 这道菜很烫，请当心。
6. 您这顿饭吃得怎么样?
7. 先生，我可以把您的盘子撤走吗?
8. 这个鱼怎么样? 我们把鱼与洋葱、辣椒及酱油一起烹饪。

II. Do you know how to set a table? Please speak out the items in the place setting.

III. Role-play

Guest:
You ordered a pancake. You want to know how to cook it. Also, ask the waiter/waitress for an extra bowl during the meal.
Waiter / Waitress:
You serve the dish for guests. You tell the guests that the pancake is made from eggs, milk and flour. It's a typical food here and very popular. Get an extra bowl for the guest.

Tips

Chinese Cuisine

Chinese cuisine is world-renowned. Generally speaking, of all China's regional cuisines, there are four major kinds of cuisine: Sichuan, Cantonese, Shandong, and Jiangsu cuisine. Among them, Sichuan cuisine is perhaps the most popular. It is famous for its hot and spicy dishes. Guandong cuisine, known as Cantonese cuisine in the West, uses a great variety of ingredients. As the climate of Guangdong is hot, the dishes are fresh, tender, and lightly seasoned. Shangdong cuisine (Lu cuisine) is best represented by its variety of seafood dishes and Shandong soups are most famous. The dishes are usually fresh, tasty, but not greasy.The main flavour of Jiangsu cuisine is sweet and dishes also have pleasant colors and pretty shapes. Because of the delicate life style around this region, people would like to process ingredients in a exquisite way.

Chinese Wine

Western Wine

Serving Wine

Scene Five

Wine Service

How to serve wine for guests?

In this unit, you will:

- Master the names of common wines.
- Practice introducing Chinese and Western wines.
- Practice serving wines.

Brainstorm:

Have you heard of "soft drink" and "hard drink"?

Warm Up

Please name the wines pictured below.

a. _____

b. _____

c. _____

d. _____

e. _____

f. _____

g. _____

h. _____

i. _____

j. _____

k. _____

l. _____

Task 1: Chinese Wine

Please listen to the dialogue and answer the following questions:

1. What are the main features of Chinese wine?
2. What types of fragrance does Chinese wine have?
3. What does the waitress say about Maotai?
4. Is rice wine popular in China?
5. What kind of rice wine does the waitress recommend to the guest?

Useful Expressions

Would you like to **order** some wine **with** your meal?
Here is our wine list, sir.
Chinese wine is often very **strong** and it has different **fragrance**.
It's **the best wine** in China.
It's **not as strong as** Maotai and it's very **popular** in the south part of China.
Would you like to **try** it?

Practice:

Please look at Chinese wines pictured below. Try to match the wine with the fragrance.

a. Thick Fragrance   b. Light fragrance   c. Rice fragrance   d. "Sauce" fragrance

a. _____ b. _____ c. _____ d. _____

Task 2: Western Wine

Now you will listen to two dialogues between a waitress and a guest. Decide whether the statements are True or False.

Dialogue 1:

1. The guest needs the wine not to be dry. _____
2. The wine recommended by the waitress is Chardonnay 1918. _____
3. The wine goes well with lobster. _____

4. Both of the guests take sherry. _____

Dialogue 2:

1. The guest wants to have a beer. _____

2. They don't have Guinness and Becks at the moment. _____

3. The guest wants to try Heineken. _____

4. The guest would like the beer with ice. _____

Useful Expressions

Have you decided on a **particular** wine?

What about Chardonnay 1981?

It is **well-balanced** and is very **dry**.

This wine **goes very well with** your lobster.

I will bring them **straight away**.

Practice:

Please explain the exact meaning of the words listed below which were often seen on the label of the wine bottles.

E	Especial	_____	F	Fine	_____
X	Extra	_____	V	Very	_____
O	Old	_____	S	Superior	_____

Task 3: Serving Wine

Listen to the dialogues and try to fill the blanks.

Waitress: Sorry to have kept you waiting. _____. Would you like to taste it?

Guest: Sure.

Waitress: How is it, sir?

Guest: It tastes good. _____.

Waitress: May I serve the wine now?

Guest: Yes, go ahead.

(... *after filling all the glasses* ...)

Waiter: _____?

Guest: Yes, it's just fine.

Waitress: So I will put the cork here. Would you like anything else, _____?

Guest: No, thanks.

Waitress: You are welcome. _____.

Useful Expressions

Sorry to **have kept** you waiting.

Would you like to **taste** it?

How is it, sir?

It **tastes** good.

May I **serve the wine** now?

Would you like anything **else**?

Practice:

Please put the following steps of serving wine in correct order.

(1) bring the wine bottle to the table.

(   ) wipe the top of the bottle with the napkin.

(   ) show the wine to the guest with the bottle label facing out.

(   ) fill the host's glass and wait for the host to taste the wine.

(   ) cut the foil wrapper and remove the foil.

(   ) serve the other guests after the host tasting the wine.

(   ) pull out the cork and put it on a plate.

Vocabulary

balance	['bæləns]	n.	平衡，均衡
beer	[bɪə(r)]	n.	啤酒
brandy	['brændi]	n.	白兰地
Burgundy	['bɜ:gəndi]	n.	（法国的）勃艮第葡萄酒
Champagne	[ʃæm'peɪn]	n.	香槟酒
Chardonnay	['ʃɑ:dəneɪ]	n.	夏敦埃酒（无甜味白葡萄酒）
dry	[draɪ]	adj.	干的，无糖的
fragrance	['freɪgrəns]	n.	芳香，香气
Guinness	['gɪnɪs]	n.	吉尼斯啤酒（英国产强性黑啤酒之一种）
Heineken	['haɪnəkən]	n.	喜力啤酒
liqueur	[lɪ'kjʊə(r)]	n.	利口酒（餐后甜酒）
lobster	['lɒbstə(r)]	n.	龙虾
Port	[pɔ:t]	n.	波特酒
rum	[rʌm]	n.	朗姆酒
sherry	['ʃeri]	n.	雪利酒
strong	[strɒŋ]	adj.	烈性的，（酒）度数比较高
taste	[teɪst]	n.	滋味；v. 品尝
vodka	['vɒdkə]	n.	伏特加酒

whiskey	['wɪskɪ]	n.	威士忌酒
Light fragrance			清香，汾香型
red wine			红葡萄酒
rice wine			米酒
Rice fragrance			米香型
Sauce fragrance			酱香型
Thick fragrance			浓香型
well-balanced			（酒）均衡度很高
white wine			白葡萄酒
wine list			酒单

Exercise

I. Please translate the following sentences:

1. 您要为您点的菜搭配些酒吗?

2. 中国的酒通常度数比较高，而且有不同香型。

3. 它不像茅台酒的度数那么高，而且在中国南方很受欢迎。

4. 先生，这是我们的酒单。

5. 这个酒的均衡度很高，而且与您的牛排很搭配。

6. 先生，这是您的酒。您要品尝一下吗?

7. 我现在可以为您倒酒了吗?

8. —— 这个酒怎么样？

   —— 这个酒味道不错。

II. Do you know the things pictured below? Can you match the words with the pictures?

wine bottle opener, cork, ice bucket, wine glass, wine list

   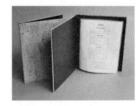 

_____ _____ _____ _____ _____

III. Role-play

Guest:

You come from Canada with a party of five and want to order Chinese wine. You ask the recommendations from the waiter and order a kind of rice wine.

Waiter / Waitress:

You explain different fragrance of Chinese wine and recommend one to the guests. Then show the wine to the guest and serve the wine for guests.

Wine Glassware Recommendations

Do you know how to recommend the glassware for each type of wine?

Tip 1: Champagne   Tip 2: Port   Tip 3: Sherry

Tip 4: Chardonnay   Tip 5: Pinot Noir   Tip 6: Reisling

Wine Tasting Tips

1. Avoid cradling the bowl of your glass which could warm the wine and change its flavor. Lift your glass by the stem.

2. Notice the color of the wine and check to be sure it's clear, not cloudy.

3. Swirl the wine a couple of times by moving the glass in a circular motion. Hold the glass by its stem and rotate your wrist so the wine climbs close to the rim.

4. Sniffing the wine's aroma and try to identify traits of wine's perfume or fragrance.

5. Take a sip, then swallow and exhale slowly through your nose and mouth to savor the wines' taste

笔记 | Notes

Part 5

Business Center
商务中心服务英语

Business Center Introduction
商务中心简介

The Business Center Department provides fax service, express mail service, telephone service and other relevant services for the guests. Hotel offers corporate travelers an array of modern conveniences including an on-site business center, a computer with Internet access, and access to copy and fax service. Hotel is also the perfect venue for guests' next special event. Teleconferencing service is available.

Main Functions of Business Center
商务中心主要功能

- Fax Service 传真服务
- Express Mail Service 快递服务
- Telephone Service 电话服务
- Internet Access 网络服务
- Copy Service 复印服务
- Typing Service 打字服务
- Secretary Service 文秘服务

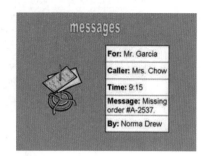

Leaving a Message

Waking-Up Call Service

IDD System

Scene One	General Switchboard

How to provide call service?

In this unit, you will:

- Practice taking a telephone message.
- Master how to provide waking-up call service.
- Describe IDD and DDD system.

Brainstorm:

What should be written when we take a telephone message?

Warm Up

Please write down the possible facilities.

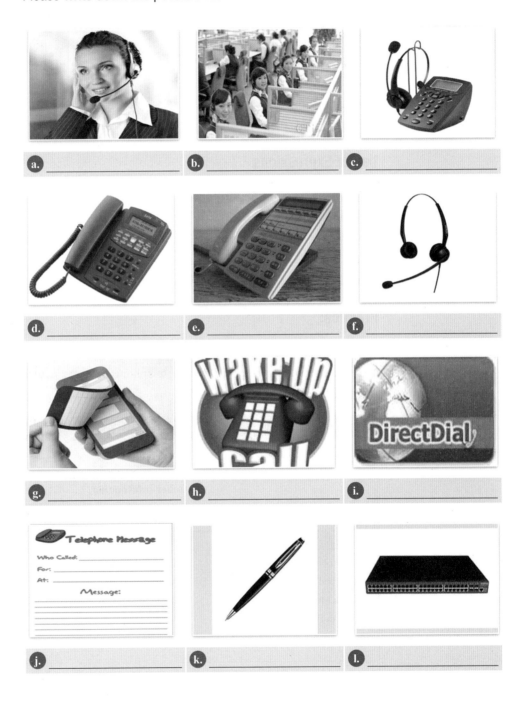

a. _____

b. _____

c. _____

d. _____

e. _____

f. _____

g. _____

h. _____

i. _____

j. _____

k. _____

l. _____

Task 1: Leaving a Message

Listen to the dialogue and try to answer the questions.

a. Whom does the caller want to speak to?

b. Which room is the guest in?

c. What's the name of the caller? Can you spell it?

d. Which company is the caller from?

e. When will the caller call again?

f. Can you write down the message?

Useful Expressions

Could you please **put me through** to him in Room 1018?

Hold on, please.

Mr. Green is **not in** at the moment.

Would you like to **leave a message?**

At what time this evening would you call again?

Practice:

Please fill in this telephone message card with your own information. Then make up a dialogue with your partner on offering telephone message service. You and your partner will be the operator and the guest in turns.

TELEPHONE MESSAGE	
For: _____	
Caller Information	
Mr. ☐ Ms. ☐ _____	
Company: _____	
Phone: _____	
☐ Called For You	☐ Please Call Back
☐ Returned Your Call	☐ Will Call Back
☐ Left a Message (below)	☐ Need to See You
☐ Sent an E-mail	☐ Sent a Fax
Message: _____	
_____	
Date: _____ Time: _____ Signed: _____	

Task 2: Waking-up Call Service

Listen to the dialogue and fill in the waking-up service form.

Waking-up Service
Guest Details
Guest's Name: _____
Room Number: _____
Call Details
Original time of wake-up call: _____
Final time of wake-up call: _____
Reason for wake-up call: _____
Other service required: _____

Listen to the dialogue again and write down the necessary information.

Operator: Good evening. What can I do for you, sir?

Guest: Good evening. This is Tom Green _____ 1018. I'm flying to Shenzhen early tomorrow morning. May I ask for a _____ tomorrow morning?

Operator: Certainly. What time would you like?

Guest: 5:30 a.m.

Operator: I see. 5:30 a.m., Mr. Green, Room 1018. _____ can I do for you?

Guest: That's all. Thank you!

Operator: You're welcome, sir.

Guest: (about half an hour later) I want to _____ my wake-up time.

Operator: Ok. _____ your room number and your name, sir?

Guest: Tom Green, in room 1018.

Operator: At what time would you like us to call you this time?

Guest: I'd like a five o'clock wake-up call tomorrow morning, please.

Operator: OK. We'll ring you up at 5:00 a.m. tomorrow.

Guest: Is there _____ to the airport that early?

Operator: Yes, there is, sir. It leaves the hotel front door _____ from 5 a.m. until 10:00 p.m. every day.

Guest: Excellent. Thanks a lot.

Operator: It's my pleasure.

(The next morning at five o'clock)

Operator: Good morning. This is your five o'clock wake-up call.

Guest: Oh, thank you. By the way, could you connect me to the room service, please?

Operator: Yes, sir. I'll _____ you right now. Wish you have a nice day.

Useful Expressions

May I **ask for** a wake-up call tomorrow morning?

At what time **would you like** us to call you this time?

We'll **ring you up** at 5:00 a.m. tomorrow.

I'd like a five o'clock wake-up call tomorrow, please.

I want to **change** my wake-up time.

Wish you have a nice day.

Practice:

Now please discuss with your partner and talk about how to ask for a wake-up call.

Task 3: IDD System

Now you will listen to a dialogue between an operator and a guest. Decide whether the statements are True or False.

1. The guest wants to call his family in San Francisco. _____

2. The guest's room is equipped with IDD and DDD system. _____

3. When call overseas, we need to first dial the country code. _____

4. The international dialing code is 00. _____

5. The rate to call USA is 1 yuan/7 seconds. _____

Useful Expressions

Can you **arrange a long-distance call** for me?

All our rooms **are equipped with** IDD system and DDD system.

You can make **IDD calls and DDD calls** from your room.

What's the rate to call USA?

Practice:

Please fill in the blanks with proper English.

Operator: Good afternoon, operator speaking. Can I help you?

Guest: Good afternoon. This is Tom Green from 1018. I'd like to call my family in New York. Can you arrange an _____(国际电话) for me?

Operator: Mr. Green, all our rooms _____(装有) IDD system and DDD system. You can call directly from your room.

Guest: Can you _____(你能告诉我如何做吗)?

Operator: Certainly, Mr. Green. To call overseas from China, you first will need to dial access code, that is 00 for international dialing code, then

_____(国家代码), area code and phone number.
That is, 00 + 1 + City Area Code + _____(您想拨的
号码).

Guest:　Okay, I see. By the way, what's the rate to call USA?

Operator:　1 yuan / 6 seconds.

Guest:　Thank you for your information.

Operator:　You are welcome.

Vocabulary

arrange	[ə'reindʒ]	v.	安排
operator	['ɔpəreitə]	n.	接线员，话务员
shuttle	['ʃʌtl]	n.	穿梭班机，公共汽车
switchboard	['switʃ,bɔ:d]	n.	配电盘，电话交换机
transfer	[træns'fə:]	v.	转乘，使转移
collect call			对方付费电话
DDD (Domestic Direct Dialing)			国内直拨电话
hold on			(打电话时用语) 别挂断
IDD (International Direct Dialing)			国际直拨长途电话
put sb. through			为 …… 接通电话
wake-up call			叫醒电话

Exercise

I. Please translate the following sentences:

1. 您能帮我接通他吗？他在 1018 房间。
2. 您想留个口信吗？
3. 明天早上我可以要求一个叫醒电话吗？
4. 这次您想我们何时给您打电话？
5. 我想要明天早上五点的叫醒服务。
6. 您能为我安排一个国际电话吗？
7. 我们所有的房间都配备了国际直拨电话系统和国内直拨电话系统。
8. 打电话到美国的资费如何？

II. Here is a dialogue about collect call with an operator. Please put the sentences in order to make the dialogue between the guest and the operator.

A = Operator　　B = Tom Green　　C = Helen Kent

(　　) **A:** Certainly. Who do you wish to call？

(　1　) **A:** Hello. Overseas operator. May I help you？

(　　) **B:** My name's Tom Green and the phone number is 259-378.

(　　) **B:** It's Helen Kent.

(　　) **B:** It's 8660-9432.

(　　) **A:** And your name and number ?

(　　) **B:** Yes. Can I make a collect call to London ?

(　　) **B:** Yes，it is.

(　　) **A:** And what's the number you are calling ?

(　　) **A:** Hold the line, please. I'll put your call through. Hello. This is the operator. You have a collect call from Tom Green in Chicago. Will you accept the charges ?

(　　) **B:** Thank you very much.

(　　) **C:** Yes，I will.

(12) **A:** I have your call on the line. Go ahead, please.

III. Role-play

Guest: You want to make a call to your business partner in another hotel. However, he is not in while you ring him. **Operator:** You ask the caller if you can take a message and try to write the message.

Tips

Sentence patterns for calling:

接电话

This is ... hotel.

May I help you?

What can I do for you?

等候

A moment, please. I will put you through.

Hang on a second, please.

Could you please hold on for a while?

Could you hold the line, please?

Would you mind holding for a minute?

如何打电话

For room-to-room calls , please dial the room number directly.

For local call, please dial 9 first and then the number.

For long distance call, please dial 9 and then the area code and the number.

For overseas call, please dial 0,then international prefix number, country code, area code and the number.国际冠码+国家代码+区域号码+电话号码

询问电话类型

Is it person-to-person call or station-to-station call?是叫人电话还是叫号电话?

Is it a collect call or a pay call?是对方付费电话还是直接付费电话?

结束通话

Is there anything else I can do for you?

Thanks for calling.

Thank you, sir. Goodbye.

Three "C"s Principles of Taking Telephone Messages

Clear

- Please write neatly to make sure it is legible if the message is handwritten.
- Explain in obvious terms what the call is about.

Concise

- Keep messages to the point.
- Make sure sentences are short and well-worded to read.

Correct

- Use proper spelling and grammar.
- Ensure names and numbers documented with 100% accuracy.

Photocopying

Sending Fax

BOOK TICKETS NOW!

Booking Tickets

Scene Two   Secretarial Services

How to provide secretarial services?

In this unit, you will:

• Practice providing photocopying service.

• Know how to send fax for guests.

• Master useful expressions of booking tickets.

Brainstorm:

What kind of secretarial services does the hotel provide?

Warm Up

Look at the pictures of office equipment in the hotel's business center. Please discuss about them and write down the possible office equipment.

a. _____ b. _____ c. _____

d. _____ e. _____ f. _____

g. _____ h. _____ i. _____

j. _____ k. _____ l. _____

Task 1: Photocopying

Listen to the dialogue and try to answer the questions.

a. How many pages is the material?

b. How many copies would the guest like?

c. Why does the guest want to make the copies a little darker?

d. How much is the copy?

e. Is the copy one-sided?

Useful Expressions

I'd like to **copy** this material.

Each one A4 **costs** one yuan.

How many copies and **what size** would you like?

Can you make it a little **darker**?

Practice:

Now please discuss with your classmates what kind of information we should know when we provide photocopying service.

Task 2: Sending Fax

Listen to the dialogue and try to fill the blanks.

Clerk: _____. Can I help you?

Guest: Yes. This is Tom Green from Room 1018. Is there _____ for me?

Clerk: A moment, please. Can you tell me _____, Mr. Green?

Guest: Yes, it's from ABC company.

Clerk: Right, Mr. Green. We've just received it.

Guest: Good. Would you please _____? Besides, I need to send a fax to San Francisco.

Clerk: No problem. Please write the _____ on the back of the paper.

Guest: Okay. How much do you charge?

Clerk: _____ it's 25 RMB per page.

Guest: Okay. Please _____.

Useful Expressions

Is there **a fax for** me?

Can you tell me **where it is from**?

We've just **received** it.

Would you please **send it to** my room?

I need to **send a fax to** San Francisco.

Please write the **fax number** on the back of the paper.

Please take it **on my account**.

Practice:

In pairs, ask and answer the following questions based on the tariff list given. Please answer with complete sentences.

a. How much do you charge for a fax?

b. Could you tell me the rate of copying?

c. What is the price for printing and typing?

d. What's the charge?

Item	Standard	Price
Printing	A4/16K/B5	3 yuan/page
	A3/B4	5 yuan/page
Copying	A4/16K/B5	1 yuan/page
	A3/B4	2 yuan/page
Typing	A4/16K/B5（The standard font size of three）	5 yuan/page
	A3/B4（The standard font size of three）	10 yuan/page
Fax	Incoming fax	5 yuan/page
	Outgoing fax (International fax are subject to long distance telephone charge）	8 yuan/page
Scanning	A4/16K/B5	5 yuan/page

Task 3: Booking Tickets

Now you will listen to a dialogue between a clerk and a guest and fill in the ticket-booking list.

Booking Tickets

Flight Details

Flight number_____　　　Ticket number_____

Departure date_____　　　Departure time_____

Destination_____　　　Total Price_____

Flight Class

(　) first class　　　　(　) business class　　　　(　) economy class

Seat

(　) window seat　　　(　) middle seat　　　(　) aisle seat

Terms of Payment

(　) pay in cash

(　) by credit card

Useful Expressions

I would like to **book a flight to Shanghai** next Wednesday.

There are two flights to Shanghai **available** on November 25th.

Which flight do you prefer?

Is the morning flight a **non-stop** one?

Would you like **first class or economy class**?

Practice:

Please fill in the blanks with proper English.

C: Good afternoon, sir. What can I do for you?

G: Good afternoon. I would like to _____(预订一张到上海的机票) next Wednesday, November 25th. Is there any flight?

C: May I have your name and room number?

G: Tom Green, Room 1018.

C: Let me see. Yes, there are two flights to Shanghai available on November 25th. One is at 8 o'clock a.m. and the other is at 5:30 in the afternoon. In addition, the 5:30 flight will be via Nanjing airport and stay there for half an hour. _____(您想要哪个航班)?

G: I'd prefer a morning flight. By the way, is the morning flight _____(直达航班)?

C: Yes, Mr. Green. CA3915 is a non-stop to Shanghai.

G: Great, I'll take it!

C: All right. _____(您想要头等舱还是经济舱)?

G: Economy class.

C: And a window seat or an aisle seat?

G: A window seat, please. How much is it?

C: 950 yuan, including the airport construction fee. Would you pay in cash or by credit card?

G: By credit card.

Vocabulary

aisle	[ail]	n.	过道
charge	[tʃɑ:dʒ]	v.	收费
considerate	[kən'sidərit]	adj.	考虑周全的
flight	[flait]	n.	航班
photocopy	['fəutəˌkɔpi:]	v.	影印

secretarial	[ˌsekrə'teərɪəl]	*adj.*	秘书的
staple	['steɪpl]	*v.*	订
tariff	['tærɪf]	*n.*	价格表
via	['vaɪə]	*prep.*	经过，通过，凭借，取道
airport construction fee			机场建设费
business class			商务舱
economy class			经济舱
first class			头等舱
in addition			另外，此外
non-stop			直达
one-sided			单方面的，一边的

Exercise

I. Please translate the following sentences:

1. 我想要复印这份材料。
2. 每张 A4 纸一元。
3. 能把颜色调深点吗？
4. 有我的传真吗？
5. 我要发份传真到旧金山。
6. 我想订张下周三到上海的机票。
7. 您想要头等舱还是经济舱？
8. 早晨的航班是直达航班吗？

II. Discuss the following ways of booking tickets and try to talk about which way is your favorite and why?

by cell phone, online, face to face, by telephone...

III. Travel the Web: A reservation staff is making a reservation on the computer now. Work with your partner and make a reservation according to the confirmation.

who, where, when, how many..., which seat/flight, ...

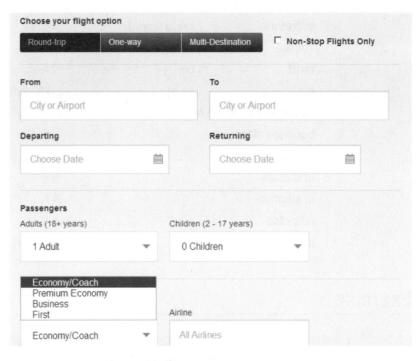

Tips

There are several useful sentences to help you.

May I have/Would you tell me ... ?

your full name	能告诉我您的全名吗？
your phone number	能告诉我您的电话号码吗？
your destination	能告诉我您的目的地吗？
your departure date	能告诉我您的出发时间吗？
your returning date	能告诉我您的返程日期吗？

What kind of flight... ?

would you like

are you looking for

will you be needing	请问您想要哪种航班？
are you interested in	
do you want	
I would like...	
a non-stop flight	我想要一个直达航班。
a one-way ticket	我想要一张单程票。
economy class	我想要经济舱。
first class	我想要头等舱。
business class	我想要商务舱。

Sightseeing Suggestions

Answering Questions

Delivery Service

| **Scene Three** | **Providing Information** |

How to provide information?

In this unit, you will:

• Practice giving sightseeing suggestions.

• Know how to answer questions.

• Master useful expressions of providing delivery service.

Brainstorm:

What kind of information is provided in the business center?

Warm Up

Look at the pictures of different buildings or road signs. Please discuss about them and write down the possible buildings.

a. _____

b. _____

c. _____

d. _____

e. _____

f. _____

g. _____

h. _____

i. _____

j. _____

k. _____

l. _____

Task 1: Sightseeing Suggestions

Listen to the dialogue and try to fill the blanks.

Scenic spots in Nanjing	Introduction
Dr. Sun Yatsen's Mausoleum	
Confucius Temple	
Xuanwu Lake	

Useful Expressions

This is **my first time to** Nanjing. Could you please **recommend** some places of interest in Nanjing?

I've **heard of** Dr. Sun Yat-sen **for ages**.

What about the Confucius Temple?

Could you give me some information about the Xuanwu Lake?

It's a wonderful place **worth visiting.**

Practice:

In pairs, ask and answer the following questions based on sightseeing suggestions given. Please answer with complete sentences.

a. Could you tell me some places of interest in Nanjing?

b. Any more places worth visiting?

c. Could you give me some information about the Confucius Temple?

Task 2: Answering Questions

Listen to the dialogue and try to fill the blanks.

C: Good afternoon. Can I help you?

G: Good afternoon. I'd like to_____. Can you recommend me some?

C: Yes. The night market at the Confucius Temple and the night market at Hunan Road are quite _____.

G: Can you give me _____ about these two night markets?

C: Hunan Road night market is _____ in the evening. It has great food, clothing stores, entertainment, and a public park attached at the end _____ the night market at the Confucius Temple provides the ultimate experience of Chinese folklore, especially around any _____. It's a great choice for an after-dinner walk.

G: It's around the _____. I'll choose to go to Confucius Temple night market to_____. Is it far from here? Can you tell me how to go there?

C: It's only 10-minute walk from here. Just go along the street, turn right at the _____ and you will see it.

Useful Expressions

Can you **recommend** me some?

Can you give me a brief introduction about these two night markets?

Hunan Road night market is **a great place to walk** in the evening.

It's **a great choice for** an after-dinner walk.

Is it far from here?

Can you **tell me how to go there**?

Just **go along** the street, **turn right** at the traffic lights and you will see it.

Practice:

Now please discuss with your classmates and talk about how to provide suggestions to the guest.

Task 3: Delivery Service

Listen to a dialogue between a clerk and a guest and try to fill the blanks.

Mail Service Information
Items mailed _____
Destination _____
Overweight _____
Postage of letter _____
Total bill _____
Way of mail _____

Useful Expressions

Can I **post** this letter to Los Angeles?

Do you want to send it **by airmail or by surface mail**?

How much does it **cost** by airmail?

It **depends on** the weight.

It's five grams **overweight**.

Practice:

Please fill in the blanks with proper English.

Clerk(C):　Good afternoon, sir. Can I help you?

Guest (G): Good afternoon. Can I _____ (邮寄这封信)to Los Angeles?

C: Yes, sir. Have you written your return address on the envelope?

G: Yes, I have.

C: Do you want to send it by _____ (航空邮件) or by surface mail?

G: By air.

C: _____ （有其他东西吗） in the envelope?

G: Yes, there are some photos in it. How much does it cost by airmail?

R: It _____ (取决于重量) (weighing on the scales) Err ... it's five grams overweight. Do you want it insured?

G: Yes, I'd like to _____ （保价） it for $50.

R: It will be $15 altogether.

G: Okay. By the way, how long will it take to get there?

R: About five days. Please _____ （贴上）this "AIR MAIL" sticker on the envelope when you send it.

G: Okay, thank you.

C: Is there anything else?

G: Yes, I'd like to buy 8 landscape postcards. How much do they cost?

C: Okay, 8 cards will be $10. The total bill for the letter and the postcards is $25.

Vocabulary

attach	[əˈtætʃ]	v.	贴上
Confucius	[kənˈfjuːʃəs]	n.	孔子
democratic	[ˌdeməˈkrætik]	adj.	民主的
entertainment	[ˌentəˈteɪnmənt]	n.	娱乐
envelope	[enˈveləp]	n.	信封；包裹
folklore	[ˈfəuklɔː]	n.	民间传说
highlight	[ˈhailait]	n.	最精彩的部分
insure	[inˈʃuə]	v.	保证，确保
knowledgeable	[ˈnɔlɪdʒəbəl]	adj.	博学的
landscape	[ˈlændskeip]	n.	风景
mausoleum	[ˌmɔːsəˈliːəm]	n.	陵墓
overweight	[ˌəuvəˈweɪt]	adj.	超重的
paste	[peist]	v.	粘贴，张贴
pavilion	[pəˈvɪliən]	n.	亭子
post	[pəust]	v.	张贴，宣布
progressive	[prəˈgresiv]	adj.	不断前进的，进步的
pursue	[pəˈsjuː]	vt.	继续，追求，进行，追捕

recommend	[ˌrekə'mend]	v.	推荐
scale	[skeil]	n.	秤
sticker	['stɪkə]	n.	张贴物
supermarket	['suːpəmɑːkɪt]	n.	超市
ultimate	['ʌltɪmət]	adj.	最后的
airmail			航空邮件
devote ... to			专心致力于,献(身)
ordinary mail			平邮
scenic spot			景点
Sun Yat-sen			孙中山

Exercise

I. Please translate the following sentences:

1. 夫子庙是游客理解中国传统文化和购物的理想之地。

2. 您能给我推荐一些南京景点吗?

3. 航空件要多少钱?

4. 超重 5 克。

5. 请把 "航空邮件" 贴在信封上。

6. 您要保价吗?

7. 您能告诉我如何到达那里吗?

8. 您能简单地给我介绍一下这两个夜市吗?

II. If you can go to a place by the following ways. Discuss these ways of going there and try to talk about which way is your favorite and why?

by bike, by bus, on foot, by car ...

III. Role-play

Guest: want to know some scenic spots of the city
show interest in one scenic spot
want to know how to get there
need to buy admission ticket
Clerk: recommend the scenic spots to the guest
provide ticket service
tell the guest how to get there

Tips

Useful Expressions to Help You Ask for Directions

be far from /be near	距离某处很远/距离某处很近
be next to	紧邻
be in the vicinity of…	邻近
be adjacent to …	邻近
be located behind/in front of	坐落在……的前面/后面
be on one's left/right	在某人的左边/右边
turn left at the first crossing	直走，第一个路口左转。
Turn right at the second traffic light	直走，第二个红绿灯右转。
go along	沿着……一直走
go straight across the yard	径直穿过院子
go back/back up	向回走
go east/west/south/north	向东/西/南/北
be the first from the left	从左数第一个
be on the corner of A street and B street	在A和B街角处

Special Services Introduction
特殊服务介绍

The aim of a hotel is to create a home away from home for all the traveling guests who need rest, food and drink. Staffs are all knowledgeable about the hotel, the nearby places, and the city. So sometimes hotel should provide some special services according to guests' needs, like entertainment service, luggage deposit service, baby-sitting service, as well as dealing with complaints from the guests.

Main Special Services:
特殊服务主要包括：

■ Entertainment Service　　　　康乐服务
■ Luggage Deposit Service　　　行李寄存服务
■ Baby-sitting Service　　　　　托婴服务
■ Dealing with Complaints　　　处理投诉

Introducing Facilities

Giving Suggestions

Shopping Center

Scene One　　Recreation Service

How to provide recreation service?

In this unit, you will:

- Know how to introduce recreational facilities in a hotel.
- Practice giving suggestions.
- Master useful expressions of shopping service.

Brainstorm:

Can you list some recreation services that the hotel provides?

Warm Up

Look at the pictures of different recreational places or services in the hotel. Please discuss about them and write down the possible recreational places or services.

a. _____

b. _____

c. _____

d. _____

e. _____

f. _____

g. _____

h. _____

i. _____

j. _____

k. _____

l. _____

Task 1: Introducing Facilities

Listen to the dialogue and try to answer the questions.

a. Why does the guest call?

b. What kind of facilities does the hotel have?

c. Will the hotel charge if the registered guests go swimming?

d. How is the swimming pool?

e. What kind of facilities does the fitness center have?

Useful Expressions

Would you please give me some **information on your facilities**?

We offer **a wide array of** recreation facilities and activities to enhance wellness, fitness or release stress.

It's free for registered guests.

Could you tell me what facilities you have?

Our fitness center is **well-equipped with** the latest recreational sports apparatus.

Practice:

Listen to the dialogue again and write down the necessary information.

C: Recreation department. Can I help you?

G: Yes. I'd like to do some _____. Would you please give me some information on your facilities?

C: We offer _____ recreation facilities and activities to enhance wellness, fitness or _____. We have a fitness center, a bowling room, a tennis court, an indoor swimming pool and so on.

G: Good. I'm _____ swimming. How is the swimming pool?

C: Our swimming pool is 30-yard with six-lane and it's free for _____.

G: Fantastic. How about the _____? Could you tell me what facilities you have?

C: Well, our fitness center is well-equipped with the latest recreational sports apparatus, such as cardio and weight equipment, bar bells, chest expander, stationary bikes that_____.

G: Is there a coach who can _____ instruction or help?

C: Yes, of course. Besides, we have full-service locker rooms with showers and saunas near the fitness center.

G: Good. I see. Thank you for your information.

Task 2: Giving Suggestions

Listen to the dialogue and try to fill the blanks.

A: Good evening, sir. Welcome.

G: Good evening. It is said sauna can _____, reduce tension and make people relaxed. I'd like to_____, but I've never experienced before. Could you please tell me something about that?

A: Certainly, sir. We _____ dry sauna and steam rooms. As it's your first time to have sauna, you may choose dry sauna as steam room is so humid that you may feel uncomfortable.

G: Great! I'll choose dry sauna. How long does it take?

A: _____, you can stay as long as you like. However, too long is not good for you.

G: How about half an hour?

A: It's okay. _____ usually spend 45 minutes.

G: What is the temperature in _____?

A: It's about 85 degrees centigrade.

G: Good. Now I know what to do. Thank you.

A: You're welcome. When you finish your sauna, you can _____.

G: Okay, thank you very much.

Useful Expressions

It is said sauna can **increase** blood circulation, **reduce** tension and make people relaxed.

We **provide** dry sauna and steam rooms.

Steam room is so humid that you may feel uncomfortable.

What is the **temperature** in sauna room?

When you finish your sauna, you can **take a massage**.

Practice:

Now please discuss with your classmates and give the conclusion on giving suggestions.

Task 3: Shopping Center

Now you will listen to a dialogue between a guest and a shopping assitant. Decide whether the statements are True or False.

1. Yunjin is Suzhou specialty. _____

2. There are three well-known brocades in China. _____

3. The guest wants to buy some Yunjin for his children. _____

4. Yuhua Stone is one of the most famous handicrafts in Nanjing. _____

5. The shopping center can ship the goods to America for guests. _____

6. Salty chicken is Nanjing's specialty. _____

Useful Expressions

Can I **be of any assistance**?

I'd like to **buy** some Nanjing **specialty for** my friends.

We **have a great variety of** goods for you to choose from.

Can you **ship** the things to America?

Practice:

Please fill in the blanks with proper English.

S: Good afternoon, sir. Can I be of any assistance?

G: Yes, I'd like to buy some _____(南京特产) for my friends.

S: This way, please. They're all here. We have _____
(种类繁多的商品)for you to choose from. Please look around.

G: What's this? It's so beautiful.

S: It's Yunjin or Nanjing cloud-pattern brocade. It is one of the three brocades well-
known in China and abroad and it is a _____(传统工艺) in
China.

G: Wonderful. I'd like to buy some for my wife. I'm sure she will like it. What are
these stones?

S: They are Yuhua Stones, one of the most famous handicrafts in Nanjing.

G: Great. I'll choose some for my children. They love stones. Besides, can you
_____(推荐一些南京美食)for
me?

S: Salty Duck is Nanjing's specialty. What about these bagged salty ducks? It's
delicious and easy to take.

G: Thank you. Can you _____(托运到美国吗)?

S: Certainly, sir. We have a very efficient shipping system. We can pack and ship
everything for you.

G: That's very nice.

Vocabulary

apparatus	[ˌæpəˈrætəs]	n.	装置，设备
brocade	[broˈked]	n.	[纺]织锦；锦缎
cardio	[ˈkɑrdɪo]	n.	有氧运动

centigrade	['sɛntɪgred]	n.	摄氏；[仪]摄氏温度
coach	[kotʃ]	n.	教练
circulation	[ˌsɜːkjə'leɪʃn]	n.	流通，循环
enhance	[ɪnhæns]	v.	提高；加强；增加
expander	[ɪkspændə]	n.	扩展器；强身器具
handicraft	['hændɪkræft]	n.	手工艺；手工艺品
humid	['hjumɪd]	adj.	潮湿的；湿润的；多湿气的
lane	[len]	n.	小巷；航线；车道
massage	[məsɑʒ]	n.	按摩；揉
recreation	[ˌrekri'eɪʃn]	n.	娱乐；消遣
release	[rɪlis]	v.	释放
sauna	['sɔnə]	n.	桑拿浴
specialty	['speʃəlti]	n.	特产；招牌菜
temperature	['tɛmprətʃə]	n.	温度
tension	['tɛnʃən]	n.	紧张，不安
wellness	['welnɪs]	n.	健康
a variety of			种种；各种各样的……
a wide array of			大量的
generally speaking			一般而言

Exercise

I. Please translate the following sentences:

1. 我们的健身中心配备了最新的休闲健身设施。
2. 我们提供许多娱乐设施和活动，增进健康或释放压力。
3. 您能给我介绍一下您的设施吗？
4. 我想买些南京特产给我的朋友们。
5. 我们有很多种类的商品供您选择。
6. 您能给我推荐一些南京特产吗？
7. 据说桑拿可以促进血液循环，减少紧张，使人放松。
8. 桑拿结束后，您可以按摩一下。

II. Look at the following chart and try to explain the items the guest shows interest in. The following sentences can help you.

Recreational items	Operating hours	Fee for usage	Services
Fitness center	07:00 – 21:00	Adults:$ 5/hour	An array of strength training equipment such as treadmills, stationary bikes, barbells, dumb bells, etc.
Swimming pool	09:00 – 20:00	$6/time	a 25-yard indoor pool with six-lane a smaller, warm-water therapeutic pool
Massage therapy	15:00 – 02:00	At least $20/time	Different kinds of massage Steam room: wet and dry saunas

The recreation is dedicated to enhancing wellness, fitness and quality of life.

The recreation center is home to a number of amenities, including a gymnasium for basketball, badminton and other sports.

You can use a wide range of sports facilities in order to get fit, loose weight or release stress.

Fitness center opens daily from 07:00 to 21:00.

From wet and dry saunas to relaxing massage therapy, our club is the place for pampering.

III. Role-play

Guest: Tom Green
Ask for a KTV room
10 people in all
Ask for some discount
Receptionist: Greet the guest
Show them to see the private room
Give them a 10% discount
Express wishes

Tips

Talking about Yoga

Yoga is a physical, mental and spiritual practice that originated in ancient India. It began as a spiritual practice but has become popular as a way of promoting physical and mental well-being.

Yoga and two practices of Chinese tai chi and qi gong, are sometimes called "meditative movement" practices. All three practices include both meditative elements and physical ones.

Yoga offers physical and mental health benefits for people of all ages. Yoga improves strength, balance and flexibility. Yoga helps relieve low-back pain and neck pain. Yoga can ease chronic diseases such as arthritis symptoms. Yoga makes people sleep better.Yoga benefits heart health.Yoga helps manage anxiety or depressive symptoms associated with difficult life situations.

Luggage Storage

Luggage Pick-Up

Valuables Storage

Scene Two

At the Cloakroom

How to deposit luggage?

In this unit, you will:

• Master useful expressions of storing luggage.

• Practice picking up luggage.

• Get familiar with the procedures of depositing valuables.

Brainstorm:

What cannot be deposited in the hotel's cloakroom?

Warm Up

Look at the pictures of different luggage and pictures related to luggage deposit in the hotel. Please discuss about them and write down the possible luggage.

a. _____

b. _____

c. _____

d. _____

e. _____

f. _____

g. _____

h. _____

i. _____

j. _____

k. _____

l. _____

Task 1: Luggage Storage

Listen to the dialogue and try to fill the blanks.

Luggage Deposit	
Guest Details	
Name _____	
Room No. _____	
Phone _____	
Deposit Details	
Piece of luggage _____	
Date for depositing _____ (D/M/Y)	
Date for drawing back _____ (D/M/Y)	
Guest's signature_____ Date _____	
Concierge's signature _____ Date _____	

Useful Expressions

You can **store** your luggage with us.

Are there any **valuables or breakables** in it?

How many pieces of luggage will you leave here?

Would you mind storing your valuables and breakables in the **safety deposit box**?

Would you please sign your name here on the **luggage deposit slip**?

Please show it when you come to **claim your luggage**.

Listen to the dialogue again and write down the necessary information.

C: Good evening, sir. Can I help you?

G: I'm going to _____ tomorrow morning. Can I store my luggage in the hotel after check-out? I won't travel back until _____, that is December 10.

C: Certainly. You can store your luggage with us without any extra charges. We offer two kinds of _____, short term luggage storage and long term luggage storage. How many pieces of luggage will you leave here?

G: A rolling suitcase and a traveling bag, altogether 2 pieces.

C: Are there any valuables or breakables in them?

G: Yes. My laptop, some cash and my passport.

C: Would you mind storing your _____ in the safety deposit box?

G: No problem. I will take them out. Thanks for your suggestion.

C: Would you show me your _____?

G: Here you are.

C: Tome Green, Room 1018, can I have your mobile phone number?

G: My cell phone number is 12340056789.

C: Okay, and you 'd like to _____ them on December 10th, am I right?

G: Yes.

C: Mr. Green. Would you please sign your name here on the _____ ?

G: Okay. Here you are.

C: Thank you, Mr. Green. Here's your receipt. Please show it when you come to _____ your luggage.

G: Okay. Thank you.

Practice:

Now please discuss with your partner and talk about how to store luggage.

Task 2: Luggage Pick-up

Listen to the conversation and answer the following questions.

a. Can the guest find his luggage tag?

b. What is the guest's tag number?

c. How many pieces of luggage does the guest have?

d. What are the features of the guest's luggage?

Useful Expressions

I'd like to **pick up** my luggage.

May I have your **luggage tag**, please?

Do you remember your **tag number**?

How many pieces have you got?

Practice:

Work in pairs. One student plays the role of a clerk at the Front Office and the other a guest. The guest tries to pick up his luggage and the clerk provides service.

Task 3: Valuables Storage

Listen to the conversation and answer the following questions.

a. What does the guest want to store?

b. Where can the guest deposit the valuables ?

c. Is it free for registered guests to store valuables?

d. Where does the clerk ask the guest to put his tickets and cash?

e. What should the guest show to the clerk if he wants to use the hotel's safety box?

Useful Expressions

You can **deposit the valuables** in the hotel's safe deposit box.

We provide **safety deposit box** for our registered guests.

Would you please **fill out** this safe deposit **application form**?

It's free for our **registered guests**.

Practice:

Please fill in the blanks with proper English.

C: Good afternoon, madam. Can I help you?

G: Yes, I was wondering _____（我是否可以）deposit my laptop, tickets and some cash here.

C: Of course, madam. We provide _____（保险箱）for our registered guests to store valuables. You can _____(寄存贵重物品) in the hotel's safe deposit box. Could you show me your room card and your identification or passport?

G: Here you are.

C: Yeah, Ms. Green. Please put your _____(车票和钱) in this envelope, seal it and sign on it.

G: No problem. Is it free?

C: Yes, it's free for our registered guests. Would you please fill out this safe deposit _____(申请表)?

G: All right.

C: This way, please, Ms. Green. Your box number is 18.

Vocabulary

claim	[kleɪm]	v.	提取
cloakroom	[ˈkləʊkruːm]	n.	衣帽间，行李寄存处
custody	[ˈkʌstədi]	n.	监管
deposit	[dɪˈpɒzɪt]	n.	寄存
liable	[ˈlaɪəbl]	adj.	有责任的；有义务的；有……倾向的
occasion	[əˈkeɪʒn]	v.	惹起，引起
storage	[ˈstɔːrɪdʒ]	n.	储藏
valuables	[ˈvæljuəblz]	n.	贵重物品
deposit slip			寄存单
go through ... formalities			办理手续
have access to			有机会接触
luggage tag			行李牌
registered guest			住店客人
safe deposit box			保险柜

Exercise

I. Please translate the following sentences:

1. 请在行李寄存单签上您的名字好吗？
2. 您要寄存几件行李？
3. 里面有什么贵重物品或易碎物品吗？
4. 我想拿我的行李。
5. 您可以把贵重物品存放在酒店的保险箱里。
6. 请您填写一下保险箱申请表好吗？
7. 我们为住店客人提供保险箱。
8. 我们提供两种行李寄存服务：短期行李寄存和长期行李寄存。

II. Here is a dialogue about luggage storage with a clerk. Please put the sentences in order to make the dialogue between the guest and the clerk.

(   ) Excuse me, where can I deposit my luggage?

(   ) Ms. Green, how many pieces of luggage do you have?

(   ) Yes, madam. You can check your luggage here.

(   ) Yes, room 1008.

(   ) Good, what should I do?

(   ) Three pieces altogether.

(   ) Ms. Green, here is your luggage check card. Please keep it, you need to show it when you come to pick up your luggage.

(   ) When will you want it?

(   ) May I have your name and room number?

(   ) In two days.

(   ) Is there any breakable or valuable in the luggage?

(   ) No, there isn't.

III. Role-play

The guest wants to deposit his valuables at the cloakroom. The receptionist provides service to the guest. Here are some sentences to help you.

☐ Safe deposit boxes are for registered guests only.

☐ Would you please tell me your name and room number?

☐ Would you please sign on the Safe Deposit Record Card?

☐ Which size box would you prefer?

☐ Please take care of the key. There will be a $200 charge should the safe deposit box key be lost. All items kept in the box will be withdrawn by the guest and the key surrendered to the hotel at the time of departure.

Sample of the Safe Deposit Box Agreement

Some Information about Luggage Storage Apps

If you're planning a trip and have a few hours to kill before check-in or after check-out and aren't able to reach another left luggage service, luggage storage apps are a great solution.

If you download the following apps, you'll be able to see the nearby hotel luggage storage locations by looking for the hotel sign at the top of the location title card. Simply choose the location that suits you best, book online, and show the hotel desk your booking confirmation when you arrive.

Receiving Complaints

Apologizing to Guests

Asking for Help

Scene Three — Handling Complaints

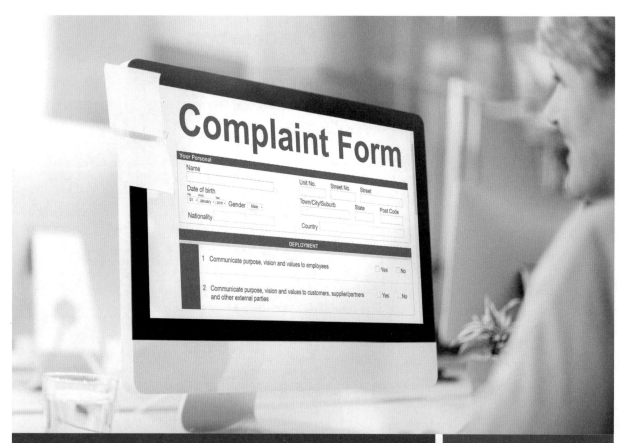

How to handle complaints?

In this unit, you will:

• Grasp skills to receive complaints from guests.

• Practice how to communicate with angry guests.

• Master useful expressions to deal with complaints.

Brainstorm:

What may cause guests to make complaints?

Warm Up

Look at the pictures related to complaints-handling in the hotel. Please discuss about them and write down steps to deal with the complaints.

a. _____

b. _____

c. _____

d. _____

e. _____

f. _____

g. _____

h. _____

i. _____

j. _____

k. _____

l. _____

Task 1: Receiving Complaints

A guest is calling to make a complaint. Listen to the dialogue and fill in the form with the information you have heard.

Guest's name:
Room No.:
Complaint:
Solution:

Useful Expressions

I'm **not happy with** my room.

May I **know what is wrong**?

I'm **awfully sorry** to hear that.

We might **overlook** some points.

I'll **arrange another comfortable room** for you at once.

Practice:

Listen to the dialogue again and try to fill the blanks.

(S= staff　G=guest)

S: Good afternoon, Front office. What can I do for you?

G: Good afternoon. This is Mr. Green from Room 902. I have just checked in and I'm not happy with my room. Can you _____ for me?

S: I'm really sorry, sir. May I know what is wrong?

G: The _____ is not clean and there is hair on the bed! I couldn't bear it.

S: I'm awfully sorry to hear that, Mr. Green. We might _____ some points. That is our responsibility. I'll _____ for you at once.

G: By the way, the room is close to the elevator so it is always noisy, would you please change a quiet room for me?

S: Certainly, sir. We'll _____. The bellman will come to carry your luggage to room 912 which is at the end of the corridor. We do _____ for the inconvenience.

G: All right. I hope I'll be able to enjoy my stay in a quiet suite and have a sound sleep.

S: Be sure. And if there is anything more you need, please let us know. Please accept my apology _____ the hotel. I assure you we will make every effort to make your evening here a pleasant one.

Task 2: Apologizing to Guests

Look at the following chart and try to make complaints between a guest and a receptionist.

Complaint	Apology	Action
This room is in a mess!	I'm terribly sorry.	I'll send someone up to clean it immediately.
This soup is disgusting!	I'm sorry to hear that.	Would you like to order something else instead?
I'm sorry to trouble you, but I don't seem to have any towels.	I do apologize for what has happened.	I'll contact housekeeping now.
The air conditioner is not working.	I'm awfully sorry.	I'll ask maintenance to see to it at once.
There's no bulb in bedside lamp.	I'm very sorry, that shouldn't happen.	I'll send someone up right away.

Useful Expressions

I'm **terribly sorry**.

I do **apologize** for what has happened.

I'm very sorry, that **shouldn't happen**.

I'm **sorry to hear** that.

I'm **awfully** sorry.

Practice:

Now please discuss with your classmates and give the conclusion on steps of handling complaints.

Task 3: Asking for Help

Now you will listen to a dialogue between a receptionist and a guest. Decide whether the statements are True or False.

1. The guest wants to have single rooms. _____

2. The guest didn't have a reservation. _____

3. There's no double room at present. _____

4. The manager provides a suite for the guest._____

5. The manager provides 10% discount for the guest. _____

Useful Expressions

I'm so **disappointed with** your hotel.

I'll **call the manager** to ask for his advice.

To **express our regret** for all the trouble, we'd like to offer you a 20% discount.

It seems **reasonable**.

Practice:

Please fill in the blanks with proper English.

R: Good afternoon, sir. Welcome to our hotel. Can I help you?

G: Yes, please. I'm Tom Green. I have reserved two double rooms a week ago.

R: Err ... Mr. Green. Let me check._____(是以您的名义预订的吗)?

G: Yes, here is the confirmation notice.

R: I'm sorry there must be some mistake. There is no _____ (预订记录).

G: No record? Impossible! I have the confirmation notice.

R: I do apologize. There must be something wrong, but we have no double room available now. How about other rooms?

G: I'm so _____ (对你们酒店很失望). I just need what I have reserved.

R: Mr. Green, would you please wait a moment? I'll _____ (打电话给经理) to ask for his advice.

G: Go ahead.

M: Good afternoon, Mr. Green, I'm the manager. Sorry to bring you inconvenience. There's a suite available. Would that be ok?

G: Well, what's the rate?

M: Well, to express our regret for all the trouble, we'd like to offer you a _____. (八折). In fact, it's the same price as what you have reserved.

G: It seems reasonable.

M: Mr. Green, I hope you can enjoy your stay here. If you need any help, don't hesitate to call us. We're always at your service.

Vocabulary

bedspread	['bedspred]	*n.*	床单
bear	[beə]	*v.*	容忍
overlook	[ˌəʊvə'lʊk]	*v.*	忽视，忽略
responsibility	[rɪˌspɒnsə'bɪləti]	*n.*	责任
corridor	['kɔrɪdɔr]	*n.*	走廊
suite	[swit]	*n.*	套房
assure	[ə'ʃʊr]	*v.*	使……放心
apologize	[ə'pɑːlədʒaɪz]	*v.*	道歉

discount	[dɪskaʊnt]	*n.*	折扣
inconvenience	[ˌɪnkən'viːnɪəns] *n.*		不方便
be disappointed with			对……失望
on behalf of			代表

Exercise

I. Please translate the following sentences:

1. 床单不干净，床上有头发！

2. 那是我们的责任。

3. 我马上给您安排一个舒适的房间。

4. 给您带来不便，我们深表歉意。

5. 我很抱歉一定是搞错了。

6. 我将打电话给经理询问他的建议。

7. 有一间套房，那可以吗？

8. 为了表达我们的歉意，我们给您打八折。

II. Work in pairs. Discuss the procedures for handling complaints with your partner and put the following steps into the correct order.

(   ) Contact the guest to assure satisfaction.

(   ) Take notes and write down the key facts.

(   ) Listen attentively with concern and sympathy.

(   ) Take immediate steps.

(   ) Apologize to the guest.

(   ) Inform the guest of the regulations about such problems.

(   ) Tell the guest what can be done and offer several options.

III. Discuss the following ways of making complaints about hotel's service and try to talk about which way is your favorite and why?

face to face,online, by telephone, by writing letter ...

Useful Tips for Dealing with Complaints

1. Try to remain calm when handling a complaint even if the customer becomes irate or indignant.

Your ultimate aim is to help the customer solve the problem, but arguing back will only make the situation worse.

2. Give a sincere apology immediately once the customer has aired his/her grievance.

An apology sometimes can placate an angry customer.

3. Resolve complaints with your initiative as quickly as possible.

Make the customer feel as if their problem is being treated as a priority, without being rushed.

4. Keep comprehensive records of all customer complaints, from the initial problem to the eventual solution.

Learn more about how to effectively identify common complaints and manage to develop an efficient complaints-resolving capability.

Dialogue-Scripts & Reference Answer
对话录音及参考答案

Part 1	Introduction to Hotels　酒店概述

Scene One	Get to Know Hotels　初识酒店

I. Brainstorm Answers

Talk about rooms, food, services, staffs, activities, location, surrounding environment, transportation, etc.

II. Warm Up

Hotel Types:

a. Motel=Motor Hotel（汽车旅馆）: a hotel with parking facilities and other services for motorists, and usually has a parking area for motor vehicles.

b. Commercial Hotel（商务酒店）: normally situated in the town center.A business hotel is a hotel that specifically caters to the needs of business customers. It usually has larger business facilities, and more conference rooms and function rooms than a hotel designed for tourists.

c. Resort Hotel（度假酒店）: usually situated at a tourist resort, by the sea or in the mountains. The hotel caters to the needs of people on holiday who stay for a longer period.

d. Airport Hotel（机场酒店）: situated near an airport. The hotel caters to the needs of airline staff and people traveling by air who only stay for one night.

e. Congress Hotel（会议酒店）: a hotel with meeting and exhibition facilities, audio-visual equipment and banquet rooms for large and small groups.

f. Health Spa（健身会所）: a hotel offering medical treatment, physical exercise and other recreational facilities.

g. Holiday Village（度假村）: a number of small individual cottages or small houses normally with cooking facilities.

h. Youth Hostel（青年旅馆）: popular among the young travelers. This hotel usually provides budget-oriented, sociable accommodation where guests can rent a bed, in a dormitory and share a bathroom, lounge and sometimes a kitchen. Rooms can be mixed or single-sex, although private rooms may also be available.

i. Inn（快捷旅馆）: Inns are general establishments or buildings where travelers can seek lodging and, usually, food and drink. They are typically located in the country or along a highway.

Task 1:

Sentences-Scripts:

a. A party of six businessmen from our company will stay in your city for a week and try to start a new cooperation with the local company.

b. We are college students and we have been hiking from Mogan Mountain. We need a cheap place where we can stay overnight.

c. I am arranging the annual conference of our international company next week.

d. Our family of 5 members are coming by RV to go camping and we would like to stop somewhere for one night. We also need to park our car.

e. I'm flying from Vancouver to Seattle in the evening and will fly to New York very early in the morning.

f. I and my friends will spend two weeks' holiday at the seaside.

Answers:

a. Commercial Hotel.

b. Youth Hostel.

c. Congress Hotel.

d. Motel.

e. Airport Hotel .

f. Resort Hotel.

Task 2:

Practice: (normally nine areas)

(1) architecture.

(2) lobby.

(3) guest room.

(4) diningroom.

(5) lounge and coffee shop.

(6) public space and facilities.

(7) service quality.

(8) kitchen.

(9) guest security.

Task 3:

Dialogue-Scripts:

Reporter: So ... How big is your hotel, Mr. Lee?

Manager: We have 578 rooms, including 386 single rooms, 160 double rooms and 32 suites.

Reporter: And what about other facilities?

Manager: The chief ones are three restaurants: a Chinese Restaurant, a Western Restaurant and a Japanese Restaurant, which are very common in China 5-star hotels. We also have a Congress Hall. There is also a big swimming pool inside the hotel, which is free for our guests.

Reporter: How about your hotel location?

Manager: The hotel enjoys the great view of overlooking a fine lake, and it's set in a large local park. It's very quiet and pleasant.

Reporter: And how do you attract the foreign visitors especially?

Manager: First, we have a natural surrounding environment. Second, we provide first-class service to create a home away from home for our guests. And third, we hold a number of special festivals to introduce Chinese traditional culture and delicious Chinese traditional food.

Reporter: Not to mention the famous health spa center.

Manager: Yes, as a matter of fact we have a very good spa center which provides wonderful facials and body treatments.

Reporter: Do you have very much going on in the evening?

Manager: Yes indeed. We offer dancing, floor shows and a nightclub.

Reporter: I see. Well, I think that's all for the moment. And we shall certainly mention your hotel in our next article on Travel Today.

Manager: I'm very pleased to hear that, and you can be sure we will make our guests very welcome.

Answers:

a. The hotel has 578 rooms, including 386 single rooms, 160 double rooms and 32 suites.

b. The chief ones are three restaurants: a Chinese Restaurant, a Western Restaurant and a Japanese Restaurant, a Congress Hall, a big swimming pool inside the hotel.

c. The hotel enjoys the great view of overlooking a fine lake, and it's set in a large local park. It's very quiet and pleasant.

d. We have a natural surrounding environment, provide first-class service to create a home away from home for our guests, and we hold a number of festivalsto introduce Chinese culture and food.

e. We have a very good spa center which provides wonderful facials and body treatments.

f. Yes. We offer dancing, floor shows and a nightclub.

Practice:

Hotel A, Hotel B, Hotel A, Hotel C, Hotel B, Hotel C

III. Exercise

Translations:

1. Different hotels meet the needs of different customers.

2. Our hotel is considered to be a Resort Hotel.

3. Our hotel is a five-star hotel.

4. There is a 24-hour room service in our hotel.

5. What kind of hotel were you thinking of ?

6. I think this one would suit you.

7. The hotel enjoys the great view of overlooking a lake.

8. We offer dancing, floor shows and a nightclub.

Discussion hotel types:

Mr. Green: Commercial Hotel.

John Smith: Youth Hostel.

Mr. Lee: Airport Hotel.

Mr., Mrs. Williams and 2 children: Resort Hotel.

Mrs. Nicole: Congress Hotel.

Logos:

a. Howard Johnson（豪生——胜腾集团）

b. Holiday Inn（假日——洲际集团）

c. Crowne Plaza（皇冠假日——洲际集团）

d. Shangri-la（香格里拉——香格里拉集团）

e. Sofitel（索菲特——雅高集团）

f. Hyatt Regency（凯悦——凯悦集团）

g. Ramada International Hotels & Resorts（华美达——胜腾集团）

h. Sheraton（喜来登——喜达屋国际酒店集团）

i. Hilton（希尔顿——希尔顿国际酒店集团）

j. Marroitt（万豪——万豪国际集团）

k. Radisson（丽笙——卡尔森酒店集团）

l. The Ritz-Carlton（丽思卡尔顿——万豪集团）

m. Kempinski（凯宾斯基——凯宾斯基酒店集团）

n. Best Western（最佳西方——最佳西方国际集团）

o. Ibis（宜必思——雅高集团）

Part 2 　　　　The Front Desk　前厅服务英语

Scene One　　　　　　　　Room Reservations

I. Brainstorm Answers

a. 临时性预订 (Advance Reservation)：
客人在即将抵达或在抵达当天进行的预订，酒店有权在下午 6 点前取消。

b. 确认类预订（Confirmed Reservation）：

酒店答应为预订者保留客房至某一时间，到了截止时间（Cut-off Time）仍未抵达并未告知酒店的，酒店有权将房间另租他人。

c. 保证类预订（Guaranteed Reservation）：

前两种都是非保证性预订。此种为客人通过使用银行信用卡、预付定金、订立合同等方式保证酒店应有的收入，同时酒店需保证提供客房，除非接到预订者取消的通知，否则即使客人未抵达，也应保证至次日结账时间为止。

d. 等待类预订（Waiting Reservation）：

是指在客房预订已满的情况下，再将一定数量的订房客人列入等候名单 (Waiting list) 如果有人取消预订，或有人提前离店，酒店就会通知等候客人来店。

II. Warm Up

Room Types:

a. Single Room（单人间）: a room assigned to one person.

b. Double Room（双人间）: a room assigned to two people.

c. Triple Room（三人间）: a room assigned to three people.

d. Queen Bedroom（大床间）: a room with a queen sized bed. May be occupied by one or more people.

e. King Bedroom（特大床间）: a room with a king sized bed. May be occupied by one or more people.

f. Twin Room（两张单人床的标间）: a room with two twin beds. May be occupied by one or more people.

g. Studio（公寓式套间）: a room with a studio bed—a couch which can be converted into a bed. May also have an additional bed.

h. Suite（套房）: A parlour or living room connected to one or more bedrooms.

i. Duplex（复式房间）: a room which is been spread on two floors connected by an internal staircase.

j. Presidential Suite（总统套房）: a suite of rooms, as in a hotel, suitable for a president or other head of state.

k. Connecting Rooms（连通房）: rooms with individual entrance doors from the outside and a connecting door between. Guests can move between rooms without going through the hallway.

l. Adjoining Rooms（相邻房）: rooms with a common wall but no connecting door.

Task 1:

Answers:

1. a double room with a bed /a queen bedroom/a king bedroom

2. a single room

3. a twin room

4. three double rooms with twin beds/2 triple rooms/six single rooms

5. a suite/a studio/a duplex

Practice: 略

Task 2:

Practice:

a. A Standard Room for 1 or 2 people costs 317 dollars, for 3 people costs 388 dollars, and for 4 people costs 406 dollars. / A Deluxe Room costs 424 dollars.

b. Yes, you can. It's RMB 317 yuan per night.

c. Yes, the rate includes breakfast./No, the rate doesn't include breakfast.

d. An "Inside Room" means the room with no windows.

e. The cheapest room for two costs 268 dollars, and it is an inside room.

Task 3:

Dialogue-Scripts:

Staff: Lake City Hotel, good morning. How may I help you?

Guest: Good morning. I'd like to book a room.

Staff: What kind of room would you like, sir? We have single rooms, double rooms, and suites.

Guest: I'd like to book a single room for Friday next week, August 4th. How much do you charge for a single room?

Staff: It's originally 488 RMB per night. And this weekend we have the discount so it will be 368 RMB.

Guest: Wow, that is great!

Staff: For how many nights, sir?

Guest: two nights.

Staff: May I know your name please, sir?

Guest: Tom Green. T-O-M, Tom. G-R-E-E-N, Green.

Staff: And your telephone number?

Guest: 206-605-0563.

Staff: Great. Let me confirm the details with you, sir. Tom Green, booked a single room for August 4th. For two nights. And your phone number is 206-605-0563. Is that correct, sir?

Guest: Good. That's all settled then?

Staff: Yes, sir. And we look forward to seeing you next Friday. Goodbye!

Guest: Bye!

Answers:

a. Reservation list

   Name :Tom Green

Phone: 206-605-0563

Arrival date: 4/8/ ...   No. of nights: 2

Departure date 6/8/ ...   No. of adults: 1

Description   No. of children: 0

▶ single room

Room rate: RMB 368/night

b. Dialogue

How may I help you

What kind of room would you like, sir

a single room for Friday next week

August 4th

It's originally 488 RMB per night.

how many nights

know your name please

telephone number

Let me confirm the details with you

look forward to seeing you next Friday

Practice:

1. Greet the guest.

2. Ask the guest for the following reservation information:

   The date of arrival and departure.

   The number of the people.

   The room type and the number of rooms.

3. Check the room availability in the computer.

4. The guest's name and telephone number.

5. Confirm the reservation.

6. Extend your wishes.

7. Form the reservation record.

III. Exercise

Translations:

1. Good morning. How may I help you?

2. What kind of room would you like, sir?

3. We have single rooms, double rooms, and suites.

4. It's originally 488 RMB per night. And this weekend we have the discount so it will be 368 RMB.

5. For how many nights, sir?

6. May I know your name please, sir?

7. And your telephone number?

8. Let me confirm the details with you, sir.

Scene Two　　Bellman Service　行李员服务

I. Brainstorm Answers

Bellman: someone employed as an errand boy and luggage carrier around hotels, often wears a uniform. Also called "bellboy", "bellhop" or "hotel porter". The job's name is derived from the fact that the hotel's front desk clerk rang a bell to summon an employee, who would "hop" (jump) to attention at the desk to receive instructions. The term "porter" is used in the United Kingdom and much of the English-speaking world. "Bellboy" or "bellhop" is an American English term. (wikipedia)

II. Warm Up

a. luggage/baggage (行李箱): Baggage or luggage means containers which hold a traveller's articles during transit.

b. suitcase (手提箱): It is often a flat, rectangular-shaped bag with rounded/square corners, either metal, hard plastic or made of cloth. It has a carrying handle on one side.

c. backpack (背包): It is also called bookbag, knapsack, packsack, pack, or bergen — is, in its simplest form, a cloth sack carried on one's back and secured with two straps that go over the shoulders.

d. briefcase (手提包): It's a narrow hard-sided box-shaped bag or case used mainly for carrying papers and other documents and equipped with a handle.

e. travel bag (旅行袋): It's usually made of cloth, having an oblong shape, and used chiefly to hold clothes.

f. luggage cart (行李车): It is a small vehicle pushed by bellmen to carry individual luggage of guests.

g. luggage tag (行李姓名牌): It is also known as baggage tags, baggage checks or luggage tickets, have traditionally been used by bus, train and airline companies to route passenger luggage that is checked on to the final destination.

h. bellman/bellhop/bellboy (行李员): It refers to the man who usually helps guests with their luggage while checking in or out.

i. trunk (汽车后备厢): It is a storage compartment of a motorcycle to store the things.

j. parking lot (停车场) It is also known as a car lot(British English: car park), and it is a cleared area that is intended for parking vehicles.

k. elevator (电梯): It is a type of vertical transport equipment that moves people or goods between floors (levels, decks) of a building.

l. luggage rack (行李架): It is a rack or carrier used for guests to put their luggage in the room.

Task 1:

<u>**Dialogue-Scripts**</u>

(1)

Bellman: Good morning. Welcome to our hotel. Are you checking in?

Guest: Yes.

Bellman: Let me help you with your baggage. How many pieces of baggage do you have?

Guest: Just these two, a suitcase and a backpack.

Bellman: This way to the Front Desk, please.

Guest: Thank you.

(2)

Bellman: Good afternoon, Madam. Welcome to Grand Hotel.

Guest: Good afternoon.

Bellman: May I help you with your luggage, madam?

Guest: Yes, please! We are a party of five.

Bellman: Ok ... Two big backpacks, a briefcase, a travel bag and a suitcase. Are these all your luggage, madam?

Guest: Yes, you are right.

Bellman: Just a moment, please. I'll get a luggage cart, madam ... Thank you for waiting. I'll show you to the front desk. This way, please.

Guest: Thank you!

Bellman: You're welcome.

(3)

Bellman: Excuse me, sir. May I help you with your luggage?

Guest: Yes, please. That's very nice of you.

Bellman: Sure...Are these all your luggage, sir? A suitcase and a piece of luggage?

Guest: Oh, one is missing. I forgot my bag in the taxi outside.

Bellman: Don't worry, sir. I will go out immediately and check ... (1 minute later ...) Excuse me, sir, is this yours?

Guests: Yes, that's great. Thank you so much for your help.

Bellman: You are welcome. By the way, the front desk is over there. Have a nice day!

Answers:

	The Number of Baggages (How many ...)	Details (What are ...)
Guest 1	2	a suitcase and a backpack
Guest 2	5	two big backpacks, a briefcase, a travel bag and a suitcase
Guest 3	3	a suitcase, a piece of luggage and a bag

Practice: 略

Task 2:

Dialogue-Scripts:

Bellman: Mr. Drops, let me help you with your luggage. Your room number, please?
Guest: Let me see ... 1388.
Bellman: Perfect, I will show you to your room.
Guest: Great, thanks.
Bellman: This way, please. Here is the elevator. Your room is on the 13th floor.
Guest: Thank you.
Bellman: You are welcome. By the way, there is a Chinese restaurant, a western restaurant, a Japanese restaurant and a coffee bar on the first floor and a business center on the second floor. The Swimming pool and Beauty Salon are on the third floor.
Guest: Sounds great.

Answers:

a. 1388.

b. on the 13th floor.

c. What are the services provided by the hotel?

1st floor: <u>a Chinese restaurant, a western restaurant, a Japanese restaurant and a coffee bar</u> .

2nd floor: <u>a business center.</u>

3rd floor: <u>a swimming pool and a Beauty Salon.</u>

Practice:

The conversation on the way from the reception to the room is important on a guest 's arrival. A deadly silence in the lift can be very embarrassing. Also it's a great chance for bellman to sell the possible services needed by different guests.

Task 3:

Dialogue-Scripts:

Bellman: Here we are. This is your room. May I have your room card, please?
Guest: Here you are.
Bellman: May I put your suitcase on this rack?
Guest: Sure, just put them here.
Bellman: Ok. Here is the directory of services in our hotel. We also have 24-hour room service. Shall I turn on the air conditioner for you now?
Guest: Yes. Thank you. Where's the price list for the mini-bar?
Bellman: It's in the drawer. Is there anything else I can do for you?

Guest: No, thanks.

Bellman: You're welcome. I hope you have a pleasant stay here.

Answers:

May I have your room card, put your suitcase on this rack, directory of services, turn on the air conditioner, drawer

Practice:

• Greet the guest.

• Help the guest with the luggage out of the car.

• Confirm the pieces of the luggage.

• Put the luggage on the luggage cart.

• Accompany the guest to the Front Office for checking in.

• Wait for the guest while he is checking in.

• Accompany the guest to the room.

• Open the door for the guest and introduce the room facilities simply.

• Extend your wishes to the guest.

III. Exercise

Translations:

1. May I help you with your luggage?

2. How many pieces of luggage do you have, sir?

3. Just a moment, please. Let me get the luggage cart for you.

4. I'll show you to the front desk.

5. Your room is on the 13th floor.

6. May I put your suitcase on this rack?

7. Here is the directory of services in our hotel.

8. There is a swimming pool, a beauty salon and a coffee bar on the first floor.

Picture Description:

a. a green silk purse

b. a black nylon backpack

c. a pink plastic handbag

d. a brown leather suitcase

e. a yellow paper bag

Role play: 略

Scene Three	Check-in 登记入住

I. Brainstorm Answers 略

II. Warm Up

a. lobby (酒店大厅)：the public entrance area of the hotel, which usually contains sitting, writing and reading areas, as well as access to other parts of the hotel.

b. brochure (酒店介绍手册)：an informative paper document (often also used for hotel advertising), that can be folded into a flyer, pamphlet or leaflet. Brochures are advertising pieces mainly used to introduce the products or services of the hotel to their guests.

c. reception desk (前台): the part of the front desk that is used to sign in or register the guests of the hotel.

d. receptionist (接待人员): a clerk who works at Front Desk in a hotel to receive or greet any visitors, guests and answer telephone calls.

e. registration form (登记表)：a form created for filling by guests online or at the front desk with their personal information such as name, birthday, occupation, phone number, home address, etc.

f. passport (护照)：A passport is a travel document, usually issued by a country's government for the purpose of international travel. It contains the holder's name, place and date of birth, photograph, signature, and other identifying information.

g. ID card (身份证): It is usually called an identity card (IC or ID card). It is issued in the form of a small, mostly standard-sized card, which usually includes full name, a portrait photo, age, birth date, address, an identification number, etc.

h. waiting list (候房名单): A waiting list is a list of names waiting for check-in.

i. signature (亲笔签名): It is a handwritten of guest's name as a proof of identity.

j. receipt (收据): A receipt is a written acknowledgment from hotel that payment has been received.

k. room card (房卡): also called "keycards", which is frequently used in hotels as an alternative to mechanical keys.

l. breakfast coupon (早餐券): It is a ticket to have breakfast in hotel, purchased by guests when check in.

Task 1:

Dialogue-Scripts

Receptionist: Good morning, madam. Welcome to the Sunshine hotel. Can I help you?

Guest: Good morning. My name is Mary Brown and I had a reservation online already. I'd like to check in.

Receptionist: Of course, Ms. Mary Brown. Could you spell your name, please?

Guest: M-A-R-Y, Mary. B-R-O-W-N, Brown.

Receptionist: One moment, please. Yes, here it is. A single room with a queen bed for 4 nights.

Guest: Yes, that's correct. Could I have a room on a higher floor, please? I don't like any noise from the ground floor.

Receptionist: Ok, Ms. Brown. There are rooms available on the 15th floor. Is it ok for you?

Guest: Yes, that's perfect. Thank you.

Receptionist: And you have already paid the deposit and room rate online, right?

Guest: Yes.

Receptionist: May I see your passport, please, Ms. Brown?

Guest: Sure. Here it is.

Receptionist: Perfect. So here is your room card. Your room number is 1569. The elevator is over there. Enjoy your stay.

Guest: Thank you.

Answers to the questions:

a. Mary Brown.

b. A single room with a queen bed.

c. 4 nights.

d. She likes the higher floor, because she doesn't like any noise from the ground floor.

e. She will pay the deposit and room rate online.

f. The room number is 1569.

Practice: 略

Task 2:

Dialogue-Scripts:

Receptionist: Good morning, madam. Welcome to Star hotel. Can I help you?

Guest: Good morning. I'd like to check in.

Receptionist: Do you have a reservation?

Guest: No. I've just arrived in this city.

Receptionist: Please wait for a moment, madam. Let me see if there are any rooms available now. So what kind of room would you like, madam?

Guest: I'd like to have a single room with queen bed, if possible.

Receptionist: Yes, there is a single room with queen bed. For how many nights, please?

Guest: Only one night. What's the room rate, please?

Receptionist: It's 459 yuan per night, including breakfast.

Guest: Very good.

Receptionist: May I see your passport, please?

Guest: Certainly. Here it is.

Receptionist: Would you please fill the registration form here?

Guest: Ok. Can I pay by credit card here?

Receptionist: Sure.

Guest: Perfect. Here you are.

Receptionist: Could you sign your name here?

Guest: Certainly.

Receptionist: Thank you, madam. Here is your room card and your breakfast coupon. Your room number is 623, on the sixth floor. The bellboy will show you up. Have a pleasant stay.

Guest: Great. Thank you!

Answers:

Welcome to Star hotel, have a reservation, there are any rooms available now, For how many nights, 459 yuan per night, Would you please fill the registration form here, Could you sign your name here, room card and your breakfast coupon, 623, pleasant stay

Practice:

• Greet the guest.

• Ask the guest whether he or she has a reservation with the hotel.

• Find out the reservation in the computer for confirmation.

• Ask the guest to show his identification.

• Ask the guest to fill in the registration form.

• Ask the guest how to make the payment.

• Form the check-in record.

• Give the room card to the guest.

• Call the bellman to show the guest to the room with baggage.

• Extend best wishes.

Task 3:

Dialogue-Scripts:

Receptionist: Good afternoon, sir. May I help you?

Guest: Yes, please. Do you have any double rooms available tonight?

Receptionist: Do you have a reservation, sir?

Guest: No, I am afraid not.

Receptionist: How many people do you have, sir?

Guest: We are a party of four.

Receptionist: Just a moment, please. I have a check ... Sorry, we have no vacant rooms for you. Our hotel holds an international conference these days and all the rooms are booked up during this week. But I can recommend you to another hotel not far from here. Maybe you can get vacant rooms there.

Guest:　　　　That sounds great. Thanks.

Receptionist: You are welcome.

Answers:

a. F　　b. T　　c. T　　d. F　　e. F

Practice:

Welcome to our hotel.

Do you have a reservation.

How many people do you have.

all the rooms are booked up

recommend you to another Hotel

III. Exercise

Translations:

1. Could you spell your name, please?

2. May I see your passport, please?

3. Here is your room card. Your room number is 1386.

4. Would you please fill the registration form?

5. Could you sign your name here?

6. Here is your room card and your breakfast coupon.

7. Sorry, we have no vacant rooms for you. All the rooms are booked up.

8. But I can recommend you to another Hotel not far from here.

Right Oder:

1, 3, 6, 7, 4, 8, 2, 11, 9, 5, 10, 12

Role play: 略

Scene Four	At Information Desk　问询服务

I. Brainstorm Answers

The guests who lost their things in the hotel should go to the hotel information desk.

II. Warm Up

a. Lost and Found（失物招领处）: It is an office in the hotel where people can go to retrieve lost articles that may have been found by others.

b. downtown (市中心)：the center of the city.

c. snack street （小吃街）: a street where traditional restaurants or food stands serving local food or local cuisine.

d. arts and crafts store (手工艺品商店): a store selling the decorative things made by hand or by simple tools. Also called handicraft or handmade.

e. Chinese massage (中式推拿): Massage involves working and acting on the body with pressure. It can be applied with the hands, fingers, elbows, knees, feet and so on which can make you feel relaxed.

f. Chinese traditional medicine store (中药店): a store selling the medicine including various forms of Chinese herbs.

g. jewelry store (珠宝店): a retail store that specializes in selling jewelry and watches.

h. acrobatics (杂技): a performance of balance and motor coordination. It can be found in many of the performing arts, and martial arts.

i. museum (博物馆)：a place that cares for a collection of artifacts and other objects of artistic, cultural, historical, or scientific importance and exhibits to the public.

j. theater center (剧院)：a place where presents plays or performance on the stag to the audience.

k. Beijing Opera （京剧）: a form of traditional Chinese theatre which combines music, vocal performance, mime, dance, and acrobatics.

l. parcel (包裹): a package sent through the mail or package delivery.

Task 1:

Dialogue-Scripts:

Clerk: Good afternoon, sir. What can I do for you?

Guest: Yes, I hope so. I lost my watch this morning.

Clerk: I'm really sorry to hear that. Do you remember the last time you had it?

Guest: I think I left it in the exercise room, but when I returned to get it, it was gone.

Clerk: Please don't worry, sir. Could you give me some information about your watch? What's the make of your watch?

Guest: Sure. It's TAG Heuer, a gift from my son.

Clerk: What color is it?

Guest: Well, it is a golden one with round plate and brand new.

Clerk: When and where did you first miss it?

Guest: This morning after breakfast in the coffee shop.

Clerk: Where had you been this morning?

Guest: The exercise room, souvenir shop and the cafe.

Clerk: May I have your name and your room number please?

Guest: Sure. Ryan Burt, in room 506.

Clerk: Don't worry, sir. We will help you find it immediately.

Guest: Thank you for your help.

Answers:

a. A watch.

b. It's TAG Heuer, a golden one with round plate and brand new.

c. This morning after breakfast in the coffee shop.

d. He has been to the exercise room, souvenir shop and the cafe.

e. Ryan Burt, in room 506.

Practice: 略

Task 2 :

Dialogue-Scripts:

Clerk: Good evening, Mr. and Mrs. Green. Have you had a good day?

Guest: Yes, thanks. Could you recommend a good Chinese restaurant in the city? We plan to have dinner out tonight.

Clerk: Well, the most famous one in the city is Red Palace restaurant on Nanda Street, but it gets very busy on weekends.

Guest: I see.

Clerk: But in fact, I think the Dragon Boat restaurant is much better choice for you. It's cheaper and closer. I would recommend that.

Guest: Sounds great. How do we get to the restaurant?

Clerk: I suggest you take a taxi and it is only minimum charge, 10 yuan. Or if you want to look around the city at night, you can also take bus No.302 and get down at Lake Station. Then, walk ahead about 20 meters, and you will find the restaurant.

Guest: Would you write the name of the restaurant in Chinese so that the taxi driver will know where to take us?

Clerk: Certainly.

Guest: Thank you very much.

Clerk: You are welcome.

Answers:

1. F   2. T   3. F   4. F   5. F

Practice:

a. turn left/turn right

b. go straight ahead

a. walk long the road

c. opposite / next to / in front of / at back of / inside / outside

d. cross / corner

Task 3:

Dialogue-Scripts:

Receptionist: Good morning. Golden Palace Hotel. May I help you?

Guest: Good afternoon. I'd like to leave a message for Ms. Susan Lee in room 638. I called her room, but no one answered.

Receptionist: Sure. May I know your name, please?

Guest: I am Martha.

Receptionist: Is that M-A-R-T-H-A?

Guest: That's correct. We will have a meeting with the delegates from Canada Trading Company this afternoon at 3:30. I will come and pick her up at 3:00 p.m.

Receptionist: Ok. Would you mind giving me your telephone number so that Mrs. Lee can call back if necessary?

Guest: Sure. My phone number is 33689901.

Receptionist: 33689901. Thank you for calling, madam. We'll tell her as soon as she comes back.

Guest: Thank you.

Receptionist: It's my pleasure.

Answers:

Message Form	
To : Ms. Susan Lee	Room No. : 638
Date: 08 / 14 / 2015	Time: 9:45 am
From: Martha	Telephone No. : 33689901
Telephone ____/____　　　Will Call Again _____	Please Call Him / Her _____
Message: There will be a meeting with the delegates from Canada Trading Company this afternoon at 3:30. Martha will come and pick you up at 3:00 p.m.	

Practice:

Would you like to leave a message for him?

May I have your number, please?

Mr. Smith in room 2609.

We'll tell him as soon as he comes back.

III. Exercise

Translations:

1. I'm really sorry to hear that. Do you remember the last time you had your wallet?

2. Could you give me some information about your watch?

3. What's the make of your luggage and what color is it?

4. We will help you find it immediately.

5. I suggest you take a taxi.

6. You can take bus No. 550 and get down at Center Station. Then, walk ahead about 5 minutes, and you will find the supermarket.

7. Would you like to leave a message for him?

8. We'll tell her as soon as she comes back.

Giving directions: 略

Discussion:

room number information, look up a telephone number, message a staying guest, give directions within a hotel, give directions to nearby or faraway location, provide information for shopping, deliver/send mails or parcels, etc.

Scene Five	Check-out 结账离开

I. Brainstorm Answers 略

II. Warm Up

a. cashier (出纳员): a person who handles the cash register at hotel.

b. ATM (自动取款机): Automatic Teller Machine.

c. POS machine (刷卡机、销售终端机): point of sale.

d. check (支票): a written order for a bank to pay a specified amount from deposited funds.

e. cash (现金): money in the physical form of currency, such as banknotes and coins.

f. debit card (借记卡): a plastic payment card that provides the cardholder electronic access to their bank account(s) at a financial institution.

g. credit card (信用卡): a method of payment that the cardholder can borrow money for payment as a cash advance.

h. American Express (美国运通卡): also known as Amex, is an American multinational financial services corporation.

i. Visa (维萨卡): an American multinational financial services corporation which facilitates electronic funds transfers throughout the world.

j. MasterCard (万事达卡): an American multinational financial services corporation.

k. deposit (押金): A deposit is money placed as a credit and it may be taken back.

l. Foreign Currency Exchange (外币兑换处): It is a place or a center that you can exchange the currencies between different countries.

Task 1:

Dialogue-Scripts:

Cashier: Good morning, sir. Can I help you?

Guest: Good morning. I'd like to check out, please.

Cashier: Certainly, sir. May I have your name and your room number, please?

Guest: Johnson Black, room 908.

Cashier: Room 908 ... Mr. Black. How was your stay?

Guest: It was great, thank you. Here is my room card.

Cashier: Fine, Mr. Black. Here is your bill. It's RMB 1384, including the breakfast you had this morning and the 10% service charge.

Guest: Let me see ... Yes, it's right.

Cashier: How do you want to pay, sir? In cash, with checks or by credit card?

Guest: I'd like to pay by my credit card.

Cashier: What kind of card do you have?

Guest: Visa card.

Cashier: Fine. May I have your card, please?

Guest: Here you are.

Cashier: Thank you. Would you please sign your name here?

Guest: All right ... Here it is.

Cashier: Thank you. Please take your credit card and keep the invoice. I hope you had a nice stay here.

Guest: Thank you very much. Bye!

Answers:

a. Johnson Black, room 908.

b. It's RMB 1384.

c. It includes the breakfast that morning and the 10% service charge.

d. Yes, he does.

e. By credit card.

f. Visa card.

Practice:

Payment Options	Advantages	Disadvantages
cash	easy to control the budget, avoid unneeded debt	limited shopping opportunities, not suitable for large purchase, security problem
traveler's checks	safe to carry, do not expire and are available in a wide range of different currencies	need to carry the receipt of purchase for the checks in a separate place to verify the check numbers if they are lost or stolen
credit cards	the most convenient way to carry, be accepted at a wide range of businesses, can access cash from ATM machines, easy to use online	may charge extra fees, easy to have debt

Task 2:

Dialogue-Scripts:

Guest: Good morning. I'd like to check out, please.

Cashier: Good morning, madam. May I have your name and your room number, please?

Guest: Mary Brown, room 4026.

Cashier: All right. May I have the room card, please?

Guest: Sure, here you are.

Cashier: You checked in on the evening of October 5th, is that right?

Guest: Yes.

Cashier: Fine, Ms. Brown. Here is your bill: three nights at RMB 468 each, breakfasts on Wednesday and Thursday morning, and a phone call. Would you please go over the bill again and see if there is anything wrong?

Guest: Sure. ... By the way, what's this for?

Cashier: Well, this is the 10% service charge.

Guest: Oh, I see ... Thanks.

Cashier: So would you like to use the same credit card you gave us when you check in?

Guest: Yes, that's right.

Cashier: Would you like to sign your name here?

Guest: Sure. Here it is.

Cashier: Thank you. There you are, Ms. Brown. See you next time. Have a safe trip home! Goodbye.

Guest: Thanks. Bye!

Answers:

check out, room 4026, evening of October 5th, RMB 468, Wednesday and Thursday morning, 10% service charge, credit card, Have a safe trip home

Practice: 略

Task 3:

Answers:

a. One night.

b. 169 dollars.

c. 195.30 dollars.

d. Yes. He will pay 30.23 dollars.

e. No, he doesn't.

f. The credit card he used at check-in is billed for the charges.

Practice:

1. Greet the guest.
2. Ask the guest's name and room number.
3. Ask the guest to give the room card back.
4. Present the bill to the guest and tell the total amount.
5. Ask the payment methods.
6. Give back the invoice and extend the wishes.

III. Exercise

Translations:

1. It's RMB 2158, including the 10% service charge.
2. How do you want to pay, sir? In cash, with checks or by credit card?
3. What kind of credit card do you have?
4. Please take your credit card and keep the invoice. I hope you had a nice stay here.
5. You checked in on the evening of August 6th, is that right?
6. Here is your bill: two nights at RMB 588 each, breakfast this morning, and two newspaper.
7. Would you please go over the bill again and see if there is anything wrong?
8. Would you like to use the same credit card you gave us when you check in?

Correct Order:

1, 4, 6, 2, 10, 7, 3, 9, 5, 8, 11, 12

Role-play: 略

Part 3　　Housekeeping Department　客房服务英语

Scene One　　Receiving Guests　迎宾服务

I. Brainstorm Answers

The duties of floor attendants are as follows: greet guests, guide guests to their rooms, introduce room facilities and hotel services, make beds, clean the room, and do turn-down service, etc.

II. Warm Up

Room Facilities:

a. safe (保险柜): strongbox where valuables can be kept safe.

b. mini-bar (小冰箱): a small private snack and beverage bar, that is defined as a fridge.

c. kettle (烧水壶): a covered container that can be used for boiling water.

d. room card (房卡): key to room.

e. temperature adjuster (温度调节器): facility to turn up/ down temperature.

f. switch (开关): a small control for an electrical device which you use to turn the device on or off.

g. desk lamp (台灯): a small electric lamp which stands on a table or other piece of furniture.

h. air-conditioner (空调): a machine which keeps the air in a building cool and dry.

i. TV (电视): a receiver that displays television images.

j. nightstand/bedside table (床头柜): a small table or cabinet designed to stand beside a bed or elsewhere in a bedroom.

k. knob (门把手): a round handle on a door or drawer which you use in order to open or close it.

l. shower (淋浴器): a device for washing yourself.

Task 1:

Dialogue-Scripts

Scene: Tom Green (G) comes out of a lift. A floor attendant (FA) meets him in the corridor.

FA: (Smiling) Good afternoon, sir. Welcome to the tenth floor. I'm the floor attendant. Can I help you with the luggage and show you to your room?

G: Yes, it's very kind of you. Here is my room card.

FA: This way, please. Room 1018 is here. (The FA opens the door, precedes the guest into the room and turns on the light) This way, please.

G: Thank you.

FA: Could I put your suitcase on the luggage rack?

G: Yes, please. When will my other luggage arrive?

FA: They will be here shortly. The bellman will take it up soon.

G: Okay. The room looks so spacious and the bed seems cozy.

FA: Yes, the comfortable bed makes waking hours fly after a tiring journey. I wish you will enjoy your stay here. If you need any help, do let us know.

G: Thank you. No problem.

Answers:

a. Room 1018.

b. According to the room card.

c. Yes.

d. He is satisfied with the room.

e. Luggage rack.

Practice: 略

Task 2:

Dialogue-Scripts:

G: It's my first time to check in at your hotel. Can you give me some information about your room facilities?

FA: Yes, all our hotel rooms are equipped with mini-bar, telephone, radio, TV, safe and Internet connection. This is bedside panel and it can get remote control of lighting, TV, and signs for "make up room" and "Do Not Disturb".

G: Great. What's this on the desk?

FA: It's hotel manual. Hotel manual gives you information about our hotel, and direction of hotel facilities.

G: Oh, I see. Then, what's this on the table?

FA: It's a kettle for you to boil some hot water in the room.

G: Thank you. What's this closet?

FA: There are mini bar and safe in it. Some popular drinks and snacks are provided on a reasonable price in the mini-bar and you can keep valuables such as laptop and iPad in the safe.

G: Well, what's this next to the door?

FA: It's a suitcase stand to hold your luggage to a comfortable height.

G: Um, I got it. Do you have trouser-press? I need to keep creases invisible.

FA: Yes. It's in this wardrobe.

G: Good. By the way, can I get WiFi in the room?

FA: Yes. Free WiFi is available in all guest rooms.

G: Thank you very much.

FA: You are welcome.

Answers:

Location	Room Facilities	Function
On the desk	hotel manual	give information about hotel, and direction of hotel facilities
On the table	kettle	boil some hot water
In the closet	mini bar and safe	provide some popular drinks and snacks & keep valuables
Next to the door	suitcase stand	hold luggage to a comfortable height
In the wardrobe	trouser-press	keep creases invisible

Answers:

check in, room facilities, are equipped with, Internet connection, Do Not Disturb, direction of hotel facilities, boil some hot water, price, keep valuables, suitcase stand, keep creases invisible, available

Practice: 略

Task 3:

Dialogue-Scripts:

G: Can you tell me how to use the safe?

O: My pleasure. First, open the safe door. When "Open" is showed on the front of the door, set the code by inputting a six-digit password. Remember this number, you'll need it to open the door again. Then, put your valuables in and close the door. Finally, turn the dial quickly, and the safe is locked.

G: Oh, I see, let me have a try. Thank you very much.

O: You're welcome.

Answers:

Please put the sentences in order：4, 1, 5, 2, 3

Practice:

how to use the safe, Remember this number, put your valuables in, let me have a try

III. Exercise

Translations:

1. Can I show you to your room?
2. The room looks so spacious and the bed seems cozy.
3. Hotel manual gives you information about our hotel, and directions of hotel facilities.
4. Can you give me some information about your room facilities?
5. All our hotel rooms are equipped with mini-bar, telephone, radio and TV.
6. Free WiFi is available in all guest rooms.
7. You can keep valuables such as laptop and iPad in the safe.
8. Can you tell me how to use the safe?

Please put the sentences in order：9, 2, 5, 4, 3, 6, 1, 8, 7

A: Good evening, madam. Welcome to the 6th floor. What can I do for you?

G: Yes. Can you show me my room?

A: My pleasure. May I have a look at your room card?

G: Yes. Here you are.

A: Ah, your room is 602. It faces the garden. It's lovely.

G: Wow, this is really what I want.

A: This way, madam, please. Let me help you with your luggage.

G: Thank you. It is very kind of you.

A: You are welcome.

Role-play: 略

Scene Two　　Chamber Service　客房服务

I. Brainstorm Answers

Yes. Housekeeping department is very important and is the backbone of a hotel. It plays an important role in keeping guest rooms clean, tidy and attractive. Without clean room and good service, the hotel will be closed.

II. Warm Up

Room Items:

a. slipper (拖鞋): loose, soft shoes worn at home.

b. tooth brush (牙刷):an oral hygiene instrument used to clean the teeth.

c. tooth paste (牙膏): a paste used with a toothbrush as an accessory to clean and maintain the aesthetics and health of teeth.

d. towel（毛巾）: a piece of thick soft cloth for drying or wiping.

e. glass (玻璃杯): a container made from glass.

f. toilet paper (厕所纸): thin soft paper that people use to clean themselves after urine or shit.

g. hair dryer (吹风机): an electric device that can blow warm air onto the hair.

h. shampoo (洗发水): a soapy liquid used for washing hair.

i. soap (肥皂): a substance used with water for washing oneself or clothes.

j. comb (梳子): a flat device with narrow pointed teeth on one edge, which you use to tidy your hair.

k. hanger (衣架): a curved piece of wood, metal, or plastic that you hang a piece of clothing on.

l. pillow (枕头): a cushion to support the head of a sleeping person.

Task 1:

Dialogue-Scripts:

A: Housekeeping. May I come in?

G: Come in, please.

A: We'd like to clean the room. Would it be convenient now, sir?

G: Yes, go ahead. I have been waiting for you. Would you please come a bit earlier next time?

A: Sorry to have kept you waiting. We usually have to clean the check-out room unless there is a request.

G: Why?

A: We need to prepare the vacant room ready for another guest. Next time, you may put the sign "Please clean it right away" on if you want your room be cleaned right away.

G: Okay, I see. When will you finish cleaning the room? My friends will come in 40 minutes.

A: No problem, sir. We'll try our best to provide a clean room in half an hour.

G: That's very kind of you.

A: We're always at your service.

Answers:

a. Check-out room.

b. Because they need to prepare the vacant room ready for another guest.

c. In half an hour.

d. His friends will come.

e. In 40 minutes.

Practice:

Cleaning order during the peak season: First, the rooms with "please clean it right away" sign, VIP rooms, then the check-out room and the last will be other guest rooms

Task 2:

Dialogue-Scripts:

A: Housekeeping. What can I do for you?

G: Yes, could you please bring me a blanket? I feel cold.

A: OK, which room are you in?

G: 1018. Besides, can you send up some more towels, please? My friends will come.

A: No problem. Is there anything in particular you need, madam?

G: Yes. Would you please bring me a sewing kit? I need to sew some buttons onto a shirt and I need some more coat hangers.

A: All right. I'll get someone to bring some up at once.

G: Thank you.

A: You're welcome.

Answers:

blanket, send up, towels, in particular, bring, coat hangers, at once

Practice: 略

Task 3:

Dialogue-Scripts

G: What's this on the bedside panel, madam?

A: It's DND button.

G: What does it mean?

A: It means "Do Not Disturb". If you need to rest in the room and won't be disturbed, you'd better turn on the "DND" sign and the room attendant won't knock at the door again.

G: Good. After a 7-hour flight journey, I want to have a good rest and won't be disturbed. I'll turn the "DND" on.

A: Wish you have a nice sleep.

G: Thank you very much.

A: You're welcome. Please call me whenever you need us.

Answers:

Please put the sentences in order：2, 4, 1, 5, 3

Practice:

Do Not Disturb，turn on，have a good rest，whenever you need us

III. Exercise

Translations:

1. We usually have to clean the check-out room unless there is a request.

2. We need to prepare the vacant room ready for another guest.

3. When will you finish cleaning the room?

4. Could you please bring me a blanket? I feel cold.

5. We need some more coat hangers.

6. I'll get someone to bring some up at once.

7. If you need to rest in the room and won't be disturbed, you'd better turn on the "Do Not Disturb" sign.

8. After a 7-hour flight journey, I want to have a good rest and won't be disturbed.

Please put the sentences in order：5, 6, 3, 8, 1, 4, 9, 2, 7

A: Housekeeping. May I come in?

G: Come in, please.

A: May I clean your room now?

G: Well, I'm a bit tired now. Can you come back later?

A: What time would you like me to come back?

G: An hour later.

A: Okay. Is there anything I can do for you before I leave?

G: Yes. I'm out of toilet paper. Would you bring me more?

A: All right, I'll get it for you right away.

Role-play: 略

Scene Three　　Laundry Service　洗衣服务

I. Brainstorm Answers

Wash, dry clean, iron, bleach, mend, etc.

II. Warm Up

Laundry Service:

a. laundry bag (洗衣袋): a bag to put dirty clothes.

b. laundry basket (洗衣篮): a basket to put dirty clothes.

c. laundry list (洗衣单): a list of articles of clothing that had been sent to be laundered.

d. dry clean (干洗): clean with chemical agents.

e. express laundry (快洗): quick washing.

f. washing machine (洗衣机): a machine used to wash clothes in.

g. iron (熨烫): press and smooth with a heated iron.

h. shirt (衬衫): a garment worn on the upper half of the body.

i. dress (裙子): a one-piece garment for a woman.

j. jeans (牛仔裤): casual trousers that are usually made of strong blue cotton cloth.

k. suit (西装):a set of garments for outerwear all of the same fabric and color.

l. sweater (毛衣): a warm knitted piece of clothing covering the upper part of body.

Task 1:

Dialogue-Scripts:

L: Housekeeping service. Can I help you?

G: Yes. This is Tom Green from room 1018. I'd like to have my suits and shirt washed. Can I get the laundry service?

L: Certainly, Mr. Green. If you have any, please leave it in the laundry bag behind the bathroom door. The laundry man will come to collect it.

G: How long does the laundry service take? I need to attend a meeting in suits tomorrow morning.

L: We provide same-day service, express service and next day service.

G: What's the difference?

L: If your laundry is received before 11:00 a.m., we will deliver it to you around 6 p.m. the same day, but if it's after 11:00 a.m., it will be sent to you next noon. Express service only takes 4 hours with extra 50% charge.

G: Ah, I see. It's only 9 a.m. I'll choose same-day service. Thanks a lot.

L: You're welcome.

Answers:

a. In the morning./ At 9 a.m.

b. Because he wants to get the laundry service.

c. Behind the bathroom door.

d. Yes.

e. Same-day service.

Task 2:

Dialogue-Scripts

L: Housekeeping. May I come in?

G: Yes, please.

L: Good morning, sir. I'm here to collect your laundry.

G: Good. It's here.

L: Have you filled in the laundry list?

G: Yes. Here it is. I want the shirt washed by hand in cold water and ironed, the suits dry-cleaned and ironed.

L: Well, sir, the shirt washed by hand in cold water and ironed, the suits dry-cleaned and ironed, 3 pieces altogether?

G: Yes, that's right.

L: Which type of laundry service will you choose? You didn't fill in the laundry list.

G: I'm sorry I forget it. Same-day service, please. Thank you very much.

L: It's my pleasure.

Answers:

collect your laundry, laundry list, washed, dry-cleaned, altogether, laundry service, Same-day service

Task 3:

Dialogue-Scripts:

H: Housekeeping. May I help you?

G: Yes. The maid has just delivered some laundry to my room, but it's not mine at all.

H: I'm sorry, sir. We'll check it right away. Would you mind telling me your room number, please?

G: Room 1018, Tom Green.

H: Mr. Green, could you please describe your laundry?

G: A black sweater and a white shirt, instead of a white sweater and a black shirt.

H: We'll bring it up to you as soon as we find it.

G: I hope you can be more careful next time.

H: Thanks for your advice and we're very sorry for the inconvenience.

Answers:

1. T 2. F 3. T 4. T

Practice:

it's not mine at all, right away, describe, instead of, inconvenience

III. Exercise

Translations:

1. If you have any, please leave it in the laundry bag behind the bathroom door.

2. We provide same-day service, express service and next day service.

3. Express service only takes 4 hours with extra 50% charge.

4. I want the shirt washed by hand in cold water and ironed.

5. Have you filled in the laundry list?

6. The maid has just delivered some laundry to my room, but it's not mine at all.

7. Could you please describe your laundry?

8. We'll bring it up to you as soon as we find it.

Dialogue-Scripts:

S=Staff   G=Guest

S: Excuse me. Do you have any laundry? The laundry man is here to collect it.

G: No, I have no laundry, thank you.

S: If you have any, please leave it in the laundry bag behind the bathroom door. The laundry man comes over to collect it every morning.

G: Thank you.

S: Please notify in the laundry list whether you need your clothes ironed, washed, dry-cleaned or mended and what time you want to get them back.

G: I see. What if there is any laundry damage? Does your hotel have a policy on dealing with it?

S: In such a case, the hotel should certainly pay for it according to our indemnity policy.

G: That sounds reasonable.

S: Don't worry, sir. The Laundry Department has wide experience in their work.

G: All right. Thank you for your information.

S: Not at all.

Answers:

1, 8, 4, 5, 9, 6, 2, 7, 3, 11, 10

Role-play: 略

Part 4 | Food & Beverage Department 餐饮服务英语

Scene One | **Table Reservations 预订餐台**

I. Brainstorm Answers

a. 面对面预订 (Face-to-face Reservation)

b. 电话预订（Telephone Reservation）

c. 传真预订（Fax Reservation）

d. 网上预订（Internet Reservation）

II. Warm Up

Services of Table Reservations :

a. Chinese Restaurant（中餐厅）: a restaurant which provides Chinese food in the hotel.

b. Western Restaurant (西餐厅): a restaurant which provides western food in the hotel.

c. Japanese Restaurant (日式餐厅): the restaurant which provides Japanese food in the hotel.

d. banquet hall (宴会厅): a room or building for the purpose of hosting a party, banquet, wedding or other reception, or other social event.

e. bar (酒吧): a place in the hotel that serves alcoholic beverages or the counter at which drinks are served.

f. private room (包间): a room especially serving for a certain group of people.

g. dinning hall (大厅): the public/common area in the hotel which serving for dinners.

h. a table for 4 (4 人座桌子): a table with 4 seats.

i. window seat (靠窗座位): a seat near the window.

j. non-smoking area (无烟区): the area where guests cannot smoke.

k. smoking area (吸烟区): the area where guests can smoke.

l. group-buying sites (团购网): web sites that can help you find daily deals and online coupons of the certain restaurant to save money.

Task 1:

Dialogue-Scripts:

Staff: Good morning. Tulip restaurant. How may I help you?

Guest: Good morning. I'd like to reserve a table for dinner tonight, please.

Staff: Certainly, sir. For how many people, please?

Guest: A party of four.

Staff: For What time, please?

Guest: Oh, we will come around here at 6:30 p.m.

Staff: I see. Would you like a table in the dinning hall or in a private room?

Guest: In the dinning hall will be fine. By the way, could you give us a table close to the window?

Staff: Certainly, sir. May I have your name and your telephone number, please?

Guest: Yes. It's Mike Williams and my number is 55564439.

Staff: All right. Your reservation is confirmed for tonight. We look forward to seeing you. Thank you for calling.

Answers:

Table No. 6
Title : Mr.
First Name: Mike   Last Name: Williams
Contact No. : 55564439
Status: RESERVED
Person No. : 4
Arrival Time: 6:30 p.m.
Note: (Special requirements, such as seats favorites, flavors, etc.)
A table close to the window in the dining hall

Practice:

1. Greet the guest with the name of your restaurant.

2. Check whether the reservation is accepted.

3. Ask the guest for the following reservation information:

   The number of the people.

   The name and telephone number of the guest.

   The time of arrival.

   Special requirements (seat favorites, flavors, etc.)

4. Confirm the reservation.

5. Extend your wishes.

Task 2:

Dialogue-Scripts:

Staff: Good afternoon. Rose Hall. May I help you?

Guest: Good afternoon. I reserved a table for 6 in your restaurant in the name of Mary about two days ago. And I have to change the table reservation.

Staff: Certainly, sir. Please wait a moment. I'll check it in the computer. Thanks for waiting. You reserved a table for 6 next Friday at 7:00 p.m., is that correct?

Guest: Right. I'd like to have the table for 10 instead of 6 and postpone the dinner until 8:30. Also, could I have a table in a private room?

Staff: Let me check the reservation list. Fortunately, we now have 3 private rooms, and one of them can seat ten at most. Would you like to take it?

Guest: Great, I will take it.

Staff: Thank you. You have booked the private room Golden Flower for 10 people next Friday at 8:30 p.m.

Guest: That's right. Thanks a lot.

Staff: It's my pleasure.

Answers:

1. F   2. T   3. F   4. F   5. T

Practice:

Guests usually change the table reservation for the following points:

table size (big/small), date or time, seat position (near the window/in the garden), area (smoking/non-smoking), room type (dining hall/private room), food (Chinese/Western/Japanese)

Task 3:

Dialogue-Scripts:

Staff: Good morning. This is Sally of the Grand hotel, Hawaii Restaurant speaking.

Guest: Good morning. I'd like to book a table for 20 in your restaurant for our company group on December 20.

Staff: Just a moment, please. I'll check our reservation list. Thanks for waiting. I'm afraid we are fully booked for that day. You know it's very busy during the peak season. Would you like to make a reservation at another restaurant in the hotel?

Guest: Oh, what a pity! Where do you recommend?

Staff: What kind of food would you prefer?

Guest: Western food.

Staff: We also have Haiti Restaurant with large private rooms for up to 20 people. And it serves western food. Would you like to make a reservation in that restaurant?

Guest: That sounds great.

Staff: Ok. Could you hold the line, please? I'll connect you.

Answers:

a table for 20

December 20

we are fully booked for that day.

What kind of food would you prefer.

large private rooms

hold the line

Practice:

1. Having a waiting area with several entertainment facilities.

2. Asking guests to leave the name, number of the people and telephone number at the front count.

3. Giving the discount if the table need to be waited for a long time.

4. Providing a small paper-like advices to notify the guests when the table is ready.

III. Exercise

Translations:

1. Would you like a table in the dinning hall or in a private room?

2. Your reservation is confirmed for tonight.

3. Thank you for calling. We look forward to seeing you.

4. Fortunately, we now have 3 private rooms, and one of them can seat ten at most.

5. I'm afraid we are fully booked for that day.

6. Would you like to make a reservation at another restaurant in the hotel?

7. We also have a Restaurant with large private rooms for up to 20 people.

8. Could you hold the line, please? I will connect you.

Dates and times:

a. September the twelfth, February the sixth, August the seventeenth, December the third

b. Monday, Wednesday, Friday, Sunday

c. eight o'clock in the morning / eight a.m.

   eleven thirty at noon / eleven thirty a.m. / half past eleven a. m.

   four ten p.m. / four ten in the afternoon

   ten forty-five in the evening / ten forty-five p.m.

Scene Two　Greeting Guests　迎客服务

I. Brainstorm Answers

when, where, which, what, how ...

Why do you think it is the best service you ever had?

What impressed you the most?

II. Warm Up

a. storekeeper (仓库保管员): a person in charge of storing and issuing food, beverages, and kitchen and dining-room supplies in a hotel food and beverage service department.

b. chef (主厨): a head cook who plans and supervises the cooking.

c. cook (厨师): a person who actually does the cooking itself.

d. waiter (男服务员): a male employee who goes to the customers' tables, takes their orders and then brings the prepared food to the tables.

e. waitress (女服务员): a female employee who goes to the customers' tables, takes their orders and then brings the prepared food to the tables.

f. captain (领班): a person who is responsible for overseeing food and beverage service on the floor.

g. busboy (餐厅勤杂工): a restaurant employee who pours water, empty astray, cleans the tables and so on.

h. wine steward (酒水服务人员): a restaurant employee who serves wines and sometimes other drinks.

i. bartender (酒吧侍者): the employee who mixes and serves drinks at a bar or in a cocktail lounge.

j. hostess (女迎宾员): a female employee who greets and seats the guests in a restaurant.

k. server (传菜员): an employee who is responsible for the delivery of dishes.

l. kitchen helper (厨房帮手 / 切菜工): an employee who does such chores as cutting up vegetables in a kitchen.

Task 1:

Dialogue-Scripts:

Dialogue 1:

Waiter: Good morning, madam.

Guest: Good morning. Just one, please.

Waiter: Just one. This way, please. Is this table all right?

Guest: That's fine. Thank you.

Dialogue 2:

Waitress: Welcome! Thank you for dining with us today. Do you have a reservation?

Guest: Yes. My name is Sean. I've reserved a private room with a table for 9 this morning.

Waitress: Please wait a moment, sir. ... Yes, we have your reservation. Shall I show you to your table now?

Guest: Sure, thank you.

Dialogue 3:

Waitress: Good evening, sir. Welcome to Rose Palace. How many people, please?

Guest: A table for 6, please.

Waitress: Do you have a reservation, sir?

Guest: No.

Waitress: Ok. Please follow me. How about that table near the window? You may enjoy the beautiful view of our city out of the window.

Guest: Sounds great! Thank you!

Answers:

Rose Palace Restaurant		
	Reservation	No
Dialogue 1	No. of People	1
	Table position	Dining Hall
	Reservation	Yes
Dialogue 2	No. of People	9
	Table position	Private Room
	Reservation	No
Dialogue 3	No. of People	6
	Table position	Dining Hall

Practice:

1. Welcome the guest.

2. Ask whether there is a reservation.

3. If there is a reservation, direct the guests to the hotel.

4. If there is no reservation, ask for the number of the guests and then direct them to a table.

Task 2:

Dialogue-Scripts:

Dialogue 1:

Waiter: Good evening, sir.

Guest: Good evening. Could you find us a table for 4?

Waiter: Certainly, sir. Do you have a reservation?

Guest: No.

Waiter: So How about the table in the corner?

Guest: Well, I'd like to enjoy the night view of the city. Could we have those seats near that window?

Waiter: I'm afraid that table is reserved for 7:00 p.m.

Guest: Oh, ok. No worries. Let's sit here.

Dialogue 2:

Waiter: Good evening, madam.

Guest: Good evening. Gee! So busy in here! Could you find me a table for 1, please?

Waiter: Sorry, I'm afraid we cannot seat you a table at the moment. Would you mind sharing a table?

Guest: Well, I don't mind.

Waiter: All right. Come with me, please.

Guest: Thank you.

Answers:

Dialogue 1:

1. Four.

2. "So How about the table in the corner?"

3. No, he doesn't.

4. "I'm afraid that table is reserved for 7:00 p.m."

Dialogue 2:

1. No. The restaurant is very busy now.

2. No. She doesn't have the reservation.

3. "Sorry, I'm afraid we cannot seat you a table at the moment. Would you mind sharing a table?"

4. No, she doesn't mind.

Practice:

a. near the window

b. in the corner

c. in the middle of

d. in the dining hall

e. in the private room

f. outside

Task 3:

Dialogue-Scripts:

Waiter: Good evening. Welcome to our restaurant.

Guest: Good evening. I'd like to have a table for five now.

Waiter: Do you have a reservation, sir?

Guest: No, we don't.

Waiter: Just a moment, please. Sorry, sir. I'm afraid all the table are taken right now and we have no seats available for you. Would you mind waiting in the lobby for a while?

Guest: Oh, god! How long will it take?

Waiter: There will be a table for five in about 20 minutes. You know that we are usually very busy during this peak season. Hope you can understand.

Guest: Ok, that's fine. We don't want to change another dinning place again in this hot weather.

Waiter: Certainly, sir. May I have your name please, sir?

Guest: Richard Williams.

Waiter: Thank you, Mr. Williams. If you don't mind, you and your friends can have some complementary drinks in the lobby first. I will inform you when we have the table soon.

Guest: That sounds great. Thank you.

Waiter: You are welcome. Hope you have a good time in our restaurant.

Answer:

have a table for five now, Just a moment, waiting in the lobby, about 20 minutes, in this hot weather, some complementary drinks, have a good time

Practice:

1. Ask the guest if he has a reservation or not.

2. If no reservation, please let the guest know that there are no seats available.

3. Tell the guest how long he will wait and try to explain the reason if necessary.

4. If the guest don't mind waiting, suggest the guest to proceed to the bar or lobby for drinks.

III. Exercise

Translations:

1. How about the table in the corner?

2. Please wait a moment, sir. Yes, we have your reservation. Shall I show you to your table now?

3. Good evening, sir. Welcome to our restaurant. How many people, please?

4. I will inform you when we have the table soon.

5. I'm afraid that table is reserved for 6:00 p.m.

6. Sorry, I'm afraid we cannot seat you a table at the moment.

7. If you don't mind, you and your friends can have some complementary drinks in the lobby first.

8. Sorry, I'm afraid we cannot seat you a table at the moment. Would you mind sharing a table?

Role-play: 略

Complete the dialogue:

Welcome to our hotel. Do you have a reservation? Would you like a table in the dinning hall or in a private room? How about that table near the window? This way, please.

Scene Three	Taking Orders 点菜服务

I. Brainstorm Answers

It is an important step in the food and beverage service. The waiter not only takes the order, but also recommends the dishes positively with the better understanding the guests' dietary habits, preference, or maybe the food character. So it is professional for a waiter/waitress to satisfy the guests with their excellent service and also increase the profit of the restaurant.

II. Warm Up

a. menu (菜单): A menu is a presentation of food and beverage offerings.

b. a la carte (单点餐): It means guests use to choose from a list of options.

c. table d'hôte (套餐): also called "set menu", in which case a pre-established sequence of courses is served, at a fixed price.

d. buffet (自助餐): Food is placed in a public area where the diners choose what they want.

e. appetizer (开胃菜): An appetizer is a small first course of an overall meal.

f. entree (主菜): food served before the main course in a multi-course meal.

g. soup (汤): A soup is a kind of food. People make soups by boiling things in water. Usually soups are classified into two main groups: clear soups and thick soups.

h. dessert (甜点): A dessert is a type of food that is eaten after lunch or dinner. It is usually a sweet food, like ice cream, cookies, and cakes.

i. seafood (海鲜): Seafood is food made from fish or other sea animals (such as shrimp and lobsters).

j. vegetable (蔬菜): A vegetable is any eatable part of a plant that does not have seed.

k. meat (肉类): Meat is animal tissue used as food.

l. drink (饮品):A drink or beverage is a liquid that you can take into your body, by using your mouth. Typical drinks for humans include water, tea, milk, coffee, juice, soft drinks and alcoholic drinks.

Task 1:

Dialogue-Scripts:

Waitress: Here is the menu, sir. Please take your time.

Guest: Thank you. Let me have a look at the menu first.

Waitress: Certainly, sir. I'll be back to take your order soon.

(2 minutes later ...)

Waitress: Are you ready to order, sir?

Guest: Well, I'm still looking at the menu. By the way, do you have the set menu for lunch? It's easier for me to order a meal for myself.

Waitress: Certainly, sir. Here it is.

Guest: I'd like to have Garlic Mushrooms with beef. Does it come with any soup?

Waitress: No, sir. It comes with fried rice.

Guest: How about sausages with potato and onion? What comes with it?

Waitress: Well, it comes with pasta and fruit salad. But you can have soup instead of salad. This one is selectable.

Guest: That's good.

Waitress: I'll make a note of it. Would you like something to drink, sir?

Guest: Just water, please.

Answers:

1. Are you ready to order, sir?

2. Table d'hôte.

3. He decides to have pasta, fruit salad, soup.

4. Yes, he is satisfied.

Practice: 略

Task 2:

Dialogue-Scripts:

Waiter: Good afternoon, madam. Are you ready to order?

Guest: Not quite. I think we need a little bit longer. What do you have for today's special?

Waiter: On the special board today we have roast salmon, vegetarian pasta and turkey sandwich.

Guest: It all sounds so nice.

Waiter: Please take your time. I'll be back in a few minutes.

(later ...)

Waiter: Excuse me, madam. May I take your order now?

Guest: Yes, please. I'd like a classic chef salad, a vegetarian pasta and a beef steak.

Waiter: Sure, madam. How would you like your steak, madam? Rare, medium or well done?

Guest:　Rare, please.

Waiter:　Excellent choice. What would you like to drink?

Guest:　Coke, please.

Waiter:　Yes, madam. Let me repeat your order. You would like a classic chef salad, a vegetarian pasta, a rare beef steak and a Coke. Is that right?

Guest:　Exactly.

Waiter:　Thank you, madam. Just a moment, please.

Answers:

1. F   2. F   3. T   4. F   5. F

Practice:

1. Welcome the guest.

2. Show the menu to the guest.

3. Wait for a few minutes.

4. Take the guest's order.

5. Introduce food and beverage.

6. Confirm the order.

Task 3:

Dialogue-Scripts:

Waitress:　Excuse me, sir. Are you ready to order now?

Guest:　Yes. We'd like to have some Chinese food. What would you recommend?

Waitress:　We serve different styles of Chinese food here. Generally speaking, Cantonese food is light and clear, Sichuan food is hot and strong, and Beijing food is a little bit heavy.

Guest:　We are not used to spicy food. Let me see ... Do you have something special?

Waitress:　If so, I suggest you have a taste of stewed beef. This stewed beef is stewed in red wine with potato and onion. And this big portion is suitable for two of you.

Guest:　Sounds great. We'll try that. Do you have any seafood?

Waitress:　How about Shrimp Soup with Cream Corn? It's sweet and delicious. It's also very popular among our guests.

Guest:　Yes, please.

Waitress:　Any drinks?

Guest:　Two glasses of water, please.

Waitress:　Certainly, sir. Just a moment, please.

Answer:

Are you ready to order now.

light and clear

hot and strong

heavy

have a taste of stewed beef

potato and onion

Two glasses of water

Practice: 略

III. Exercise

Translations:

1. Are you ready to order, sir? / May I take your order now?

2. Please take your time. I'll be back in a few minutes.

3. On the special board today we have beef steak, shrimp soup and turkey sandwich.

4. How would you like your steak? Rare, medium or well done?

5. What would you like to drink?

6. We serve different styles of Chinese food here.

7. This big portion is suitable for two of you.

8. How about Mashroom Soup with Cream? It's also very popular among our guests.

Please give the recommendations to guests according to their needs.

1. seafood

2. vegetarian food

3. set meal

4. fast food

5. buffet

Role-play: 略

Scene Four	Serving Dishes　席间服务

I. Brainstorm Answers

It's very important for a waiter/waitress to understand the menu. Different menus use different words to mean the same thing. They also use certain words to make food sound more delicious. Knowing more about the menu can make you serve your guests promptly and accurately.

II. Warm Up

The items used on the dining table:

a. teapot (茶壶): A teapot is a vessel used for serving tea.

b. glass (杯子): A glass is a container made of glass and used to drink.

c.knife (餐刀): A knife means a tool for cutting.

d. fork (叉子): A fork is a tool consisting of a handle with several narrow tines on one end for eating in western countries.

e. spoon (餐勺): A spoon is a tool consisting of a small shallow bowl, oval or round, at the end of a handle. It's used for measure, mix, stir or hold food.

f. bowl (碗):A bowl is a round, open-top container used in many cultures to serve hot and cold food.

g. plate (盘子): A plate is a broad, mainly flat vessel commonly used to serve food.

h. tablecloth (餐桌布): A tablecloth is a cloth used to cover a table.

i. tray(托盘): A tray is a shallow platform designed for carrying things like dish plates.

j. napkin (餐巾纸): A napkin is a rectangle of cloth used at the table for wiping the mouth and fingers while eating.

k. coaster (杯托): A coaster is an article used to rest beverages upon.

l. placemat (餐具垫):A placemat or table mat is a covering and/or pad designating an individual place setting and used to protect the dinner table from water marks, food stains or heat damage.

Task 1:

Dialogue-Scripts:

Waitress: Excuse me, sir. May I serve the dish now?

Guest: Sure.

Waitress: Here is your food, Sweet and Sour Chicken. Please enjoy it.

Guest: Wow, it looks nice. How do you cook it?

Waitress: We cook the chicken with black rice vinegar, eggs, soy sauce, and pepper. It looks good, smells good and tastes good.

Guest: What part of chicken did the chef use in it?

Waitress: Boneless and skinless chicken breasts.

Guest: Em ... It sounds great.

Waitress: I hope all of you enjoy your food.

Answers:

1. "Excuse me, sir. May I serve the dish now?"

2. Sweet and Sour Chicken.

3. The ingredients are chicken, black rice vinegar, eggs, soy sauce, and pepper.

4. It looks good, smells good and tastes good.

5. Boneless and skinless chicken breasts.

Practice: 略

Task 2:

Dialogue-Scripts:

Waitress: Sorry to disturb you, sir. May I move this dish to serve the soup?

Guest: Sure. Go ahead.

Waitress: This is very hot, please be careful.

Guest: Thank you.

Waitress: Would you like me to separate the soup for you?

Guest: Yes, please.

Waitress: Certainly, sir. ... Well, the soup is ready, please enjoy!

Guest 1: By the way, would you give me some more napkins, please?

Waitress: Certainly, sir. I will bring you some more.

Guest 2: Also, I am not very good at using chopsticks. Can you bring me a knife and a fork?

Waiter: No problem. I will be back soon.

Answers:

move this dish to serve the soup

This is very hot.

the soup is ready

I will bring you some more.

a knife and a fork

Practice: 略

Task 3:

Dialogue-Scripts:

Dialogue 1: Asking about the dish

Waitress: Are you enjoy your meal?

Guest: Yes, it's very delicious. Thank you.

Waitress: May I take your plate, sir?

Guest: Sure.

Waitress: How is the fish?

Guest: Well, it is very tasty, but a little bit spicy.

Waitress: The fish you ordered is a typical Sichuan food which is famous but very hot. Maybe next time you could try Shanghai food, it's not very hot and a little bit sweet.

Guest: Really? I will try that next time. Thank you!

Waitress: Just let me know if you need any help.

Dialogue 2: Asking guests to pay the bill

Waitress: Excuse me, sir. Do you need anything else? If not, do you mind if I bring you the bill? It's nearly closing time.

Guest: Ok. Can I have the bill?

Waitress: Here it is, sir. Your bill totals 484 yuan, including service charge.

Guest: Can I use my credit card here?

Waitress: Yes, sir. What kind have you got?

Guest: Visa card.

Waitress: That'll be fine.

Answers:

Dialogue 1:

1. F   2. F   3. T   4. F

Dialogue 2:

1. T   2. F   3. F   4. T

Practice:

1. Would you like to see the dessert menu?

2. How is the soup?

3. Can I get you a coffee or a tea?

4. May I take the plate, sir/madam?

III. Exercise

Translations:

1. May I serve the dish now?

2. It looks good, smells good and tastes good.

3. I hope all of you enjoy your food.

4. May I move this dish to serve the soup?

5. This is very hot, please be careful.

6. Are you enjoy your meal?

7. May I take your plate, sir?

8. How is the fish? We cook the fish with onion, pepper and soy sauce.

Table setting:

(from left to right each line)

bread and butter plate, water glass, salad fork, dinner fork, plates, napkin, dinner knife, soup spoon, tea spoon

Role-play: 略

Scene Five	Wine Service 酒水服务

I. Brainstorm Answers

Drinks, or beverages, includes juice, soft drinks, and carbonated drinks, have some form of water in them, water itself is often not classified as a beverage. It's decided into "soft drinks" and "hard drinks". Soft drinks may contain less than 0.5% alcohol or no alcohol at all, while hard drinks usually contain much more alcohol.

II. Warm Up

The wines:

a. Port (波特酒): It is typically a sweet, red wine, often served as a dessert wine.

b. sherry (雪利酒): It is a fortified wine made from white grapes that are grown in Spain.

c. Champagne (香槟酒): It is a sparkling wine produced from grapes grown in the Champagne region of France.

d. vodka (伏特加): It is a distilled beverage and commonly used in cocktails and mixed drinks.

e. rum (朗姆酒): It is a distilled alcoholic beverage.

f. beer (啤酒): It is a very common alcoholic beverage.

g. brandy (白兰地): It is a spirit produced by distilling wine. Brandy generally contains 35% ~60% alcohol by volume and is typically taken as an after-dinner drink.

h. whiskey (威士忌): It is a type of distilled alcoholic beverage made from fermented grain mash.

i. red wine (红葡萄酒): It is a type of wine made from dark-coloured (black) grapes.

j. white wine (白葡萄酒): It is a wine whose color can be straw-yellow, yellow-green, or yellow-gold.

k. liqueur (利口酒): It is an alcoholic beverage made from a distilled spirit that has been flavored with fruit, cream, herbs, spices, flowers or nuts and bottled with added sugar.

l. rice wine (米酒、白酒): It is the eastern alcoholic beverage made from rice, originated from China.

Task 1:

Dialogue-Scripts:

Waitress: Good evening, sir. Would you like to order some wine with your meal?

Guest: Yes.

Waitress: Here is our wine list, sir.

Guest: Thank you. Frankly speaking, I don't know much about Chinese wine.

Could you make some recommendations?

Waitress: Well, Chinese wine is often very strong and it has different fragrance, such as Sauce fragrance, Thick fragrance, Light fragrance, Rice fragrance and so on. The most popular one in China is called Maotai and it's a kind of Sauce fragrance. It's the best wine in China.

Guest: Thank you, but I think I will try it next time. What other Chinese wine, please? I heard the rice wine is special in China.

Waitress: Yes. We also have Shaoxing rice wine, and Shaoxing is the famous wine making city in China. It's not as strong as Maotai and it's very popular in the south part of China. Would you like to try it?

Guest: It sounds interesting. Yes, I will try it.

Answers:

1. Chinese wine is often very strong and it has different fragrance.

2. Chinese wine has different fragrance, such as Sauce fragrance, Thick fragrance, Light fragrance, Rice fragrance and so on.

3. The most popular one in China is called Maotai and it's a kind of Sauce fragrance. It's the best wine in China.

4. Yes.

5. We also have Shaoxing rice wine, and Shaoxing is the famous wine making city in China. It's not as strong as Maotai and it's very popular in the south part of China.

Practice:

a.   d.   b.   c.

Task 2:

Dialogue-Scripts:

Dialogue 1:

Waitress: Excuse me, sir. Have you decided on a particular wine?

Guest: You've got quite a selection here. Any recommendations? We'd like one which is very dry.

Waitress: Certainly, sir. What about Chardonnay 1981? It is well-balanced and is very dry. And this wine goes very well with your lobster.

Guest: That sounds great! So I will try the Chardonnay and my wife will take sherry.

Waitress: Certainly, sir. I will bring them straight away.

Dialogue 2:

Waitress: What can I do for you, sir?

Guest: Can I have a beer, please?

Waitress: Sure. What brand of beer would you prefer?

Guest: I'll take a Guinness, please.

Waitress: I am sorry, sir. We don't have any Guinness at the moment, but we do have Becks or Heineken. Would you like to try it?

Guest: That's fine. I will take Becks.

Waitress: Would you like your beer with ice?

Guest: Yes, please.

Waitress: Certainly, sir. Just a moment, please.

sAnswers:

Dialogue 1:

1. F　　2. F　　3. T　　4. F

Dialogue 2:

1. T　　2. F　　3. F　　4. T

Practice: 略

E	Especial	特制的	F	Fine	优良的
X	Extra	特别的	V	Very	十分
O	Old	年代久的	S	Superior	上好的

Task 3:

Dialogue-Scripts:

Waitress: Sorry to have kept you waiting. Here is your Burgundy, sir. Would you like to taste it?

Guest: Sure.

Waitress: How is it, sir?

Guest: It tastes good. The wine is excellent.

Waitress: May I serve the wine now?

Guest: Yes, go ahead.

(after filling all the glasses)

Waitress: Will this be all right?

Guest: Yes, it's just fine.

Waitress: So I will put the cork here. Would you like anything else, tea, coffee or water?

Guest: No, thanks.

Waitress: You are welcome. Please enjoy your meal.

Answers:

Here is your Burgundy, sir.

The wine is excellent.

Will this be all right?

tea, coffee or water

Please enjoy your meal.

Practice:

1, 4, 2, 6, 3, 7, 5

III. Exercise

Translations:

1. Would you like to order some wine with your meal?

2. Chinese wine is often very strong and it has different fragrance.

3. It's not as strong as Maotai and it's very popular in the south part of China.

4. Here is our wine list, sir.

5. This wine is well-balanced and goes very well with your steak.

6. Here is your wine, sir. Would you like to taste it?

7. May I serve the wine now?

8. — How is the wine, sir?

　　— It tastes good.

Match the pictures: (From the left to right)

cork, wine glass, wine bottle opener, wine list, ice bucket

Role-play: 略

Part 5	Business Center　商务中心服务英语

Scene One	General Switchboard　通信服务

I. Brainstorm Answers

Caller's name, time, reason to call, etc.

II. Warm Up

General Switchboard:

a. operator (话务员): a person who connects telephone calls at a telephone exchange or in a place such as an office or hotel.

b. call center (话务中心): a centralized office used for receiving or transmitting a large volume of requests by telephone.

c. telephone (电话机): the electrical system of communication that you use to talk directly to someone else in a different place.

d. outside line (外线电话): telephone which can dial long-distance call.

e. inside line (内线电话): phones made between the same company.

f. headset (话务耳麦): a small pair of headphones that you can use for listening to a radio or recorded music, or for using a telephone.

g. sticker (便签纸): a small piece of paper or plastic, with writing or a picture on one side, which you can stick onto a surface.

h. wake up call (叫醒电话): call to make sb. awake.

i. IDD (国际长途直拨): international direct dial.

j. telephone message card (电话留言卡): paper that can be written some information for telephone message.

k. pen (钢笔): a long thin object which you use to write in ink.

l. switchboard (交换机): a place in a large office or business where all the telephone calls are connected.

Task 1:

Dialogue-Scripts:

O: Lake City Hotel. Operator. May I help you?

G: I'd like to speak to Mr. Tom Green. Could you please put me through to him in Room 1018?

O: Certainly, sir. Hold on, please ... Thank you for waiting, sir. Mr. Green is not in at the moment. Would you like to leave a message?

G: OK. Tell him I'll call him again this evening.

O: May I have your name, sir?

G: George Wilson from ABC Company. G-e-o-r-g-e, George, W-i-l-s-o-n, Wilson.

O: Thank you, Mr. Wilson. At what time this evening would you call again ?

G: About eight.

O: Mr. George Wilson will call Mr. Tom Green again at eight this evening. Is that right?

G: Yeah .Thank you. Goodbye.

Answers:

a. Mr. Tom Green.

b. Room 1018.

c. George Wilson .G-e-o-r-g-e, George, W-i-l-s-o-n, Wilson.

d. ABC Company.

e. About eight this evening.

f. Mr. George Wilson will call Mr. Tom Green again at eight this evening.

Practice: 略

Task 2:

Dialogue-Scripts:

Operator: Good evening. What can I do for you, sir?

Guest: Good evening. This is Tom Green calling from 1018. I'm flying to Shenzhen early tomorrow morning. May I ask for a wake-up call tomorrow morning?

Operator: Certainly. What time would you like?

Guest: 5:30 a.m.

Operator: I see. 5:30 a.m., Mr. Green, room 1018. Anything else can I do for you?

Guest: That's all. Thank you!

Operator: You are welcome, sir.

Guest: (about half an hour later) I want to change my wake-up time.

Operator: Ok. May I know your room number and your name, sir?

Guest: Tom Green, in room 1018.

Operator: At what time would you like us to call you this time?

Guest: I'd like a five o'clock wake-up call tomorrow morning, please.

Operator: OK. We'll ring you up at 5:00 a.m. tomorrow.

Guest: Is there a shuttle bus to the airport that early?

Operator: Yes, there is, sir. It leaves the hotel front door every half an hour from 5 a.m. until 10:00 p.m. every day.

Guest: Excellent. Thanks a lot.

Operator: It's my pleasure.

(The next morning at five o'clock)

Operator: Good morning. This is your five o'clock wake-up call.

Guest: Oh, thank you. By the way, could you connect me to the room service, please?

Operator: Yes, sir. I'll transfer you right now. Wish you have a nice day. Goodbye!

Guest: Bye!

Waking-up Service

Guest Details

Guest's Name: Tom Green

Room Number: 1018

Call Details

Original time of wake-up call: <u>5:30 a.m.</u>

Final time of wake-up call: <u>five o'clock</u>

Reason for wake-up call: <u>catch flight to Shenzhen</u>

Other service required: <u>room service</u>

Answers:

calling from, wake-up call, Anything else, change, May I know a shuttle bus, every half an hour, transfer

Practice: 略

Task 3:

Dialogue-Scripts:

O: Good afternoon, operator speaking. Can I help you?

G: Good afternoon. This is Tom Green from 1018. I'd like to call my family in New York. Can you arrange an international call for me?

O: Mr. Green, all our rooms are equipped with IDD system and DDD system. You can call directly from your room.

G: Oh, can you tell me how to do that?

O: Certainly, Mr. Green. To call overseas from China, you first will need to dial access code, that is 00 for international dialing code, then your country code, area code and phone number. That is, 00 + 1 + City Area Code + Phone Number you wish to call.

G: Okay, I see. By the way, what's the rate to call USA?

O: 1 yuan / 6 seconds.

G: Thank you for your information.

O: You are welcome.

Answers:

1. F   2. T   3. F   4. T   5. F

Practice:

international call, are equipped with, tell me how to do that, your country code, Phone Number you wish to call

III. Exercise

Translations:

1. Could you please put me through to him in Room 1018?

2. Would you like to leave a message?

3. May I ask for a wake-up call tomorrow morning?

4. At what time would you like us to call you this time?

5. I'd like a five o'clock wake-up call tomorrow morning, please.

6. Can you arrange an international call for me?

7. All our rooms are equipped with IDD system and DDD system.

8. What's the rate to call USA?

Answers:

3,1,8,4,6,7,2,11,5,9,13,10,12

Role-play: 略

Scene Two   Secretarial Services   文秘服务

I. Brainstorm Answers

Typing, printing, photocopy, sending fax, scanning, translation, booking tickets, etc.

II. Warm Up

Office Equipment:

a. fax (传真机): a piece of equipment used to copy documents by sending information electronically along a telephone line, and to receive copies that are sent in this way.

b. printer (打印机): a machine that can be connected to a computer in order to make copies on paper of documents or other information held by the computer.

c. duplicator (复印机): apparatus that makes copies of typed, written or drawn material.

d. scanner (扫描仪): a piece of computer equipment that you use for copying a picture or document onto a computer.

e. coffee maker (咖啡机): an appliance for brewing coffee automatically.

f. laptop (笔记本电脑): a small portable computer.

g. iPad: a kind of electronical facility.

h. claw/nail puller (起钉器): a mechanical device that is curved or bent to suspend or hold or pull something.

i. computer (电脑): an electronic machine that can store and deal with large amounts of information.

j. paper shredder (碎纸机): a mechanical device used to cut paper into chad.

k. bill counter (点钞机): a machine which can count money.

l. stapler (订书机): a device used for putting staples into sheets of paper.

Task 1:

Dialogue-Scripts:

C: Good afternoon, sir. Can I help you?

G: Yes, I'd like to copy this material of 15 pages.

C: Okay. How many copies and what size would you like?

G: Three copies of each. A4 size, please. Can you make it a little darker? The original is a little light.

C: No problem. Is this okay?

G: Good. Thank you very much.

C: It's my pleasure. Which do you prefer, both-sided or one-sided?

G: One-sided, please.

C: Sorry to have kept you waiting. Would you like me to staple these for you?

G: You're very considerate. How much is it?

C: Each one A4 costs one yuan. It comes to 45 yuan.

Answers:

a. 15 pages.

b. 3 copies.

c. The original is a little light.

d. 45 yuan.

e. Yes.

Practice: 略

Task 2:

Dialogue-Scripts:

C: Business center. Can I help you?

G: Yes. This is Tom Green from Room 1018. Is there a fax for me?

C: A moment, please. Can you tell me where it is from, Mr. Green?

G: Yes, it's from ABC company.

C: Right, Mr. Green. We've just received it.

G: Good. Would you please send it to my room? Besides, I need to send a fax to San-Francisco.

C: No problem. Please write the fax number on the back of the paper.

G: Okay. How much do you charge?

C: To overseas it's 25 RMB per page.

G: Okay. Please take it on my account.

Answers:

Business center, a fax, where it is from, send it to my room, fax number, To overseas, take it on my account

Practice: 略

Task 3:

Dialogue-Scripts:

Clerk: Good afternoon, sir. What can I do for you?

Guest: Good afternoon. I would like to book a flight to Shanghai next Wednesday, November 25th. Is there any flight?

Clerk: May I have your name and room number?

Guest: Tom Green, room 1018.

Clerk: Let me see. Yes, there are two flights to Shanghai available on November 25th. One is at 8 o'clock a.m. and the other is at 5:30 in the afternoon. In addition, the 5:30 flight will be via Nanjing airport and stay there for half an hour. Which flight do you prefer?

Guest: I'd prefer a morning flight. By the way, is the morning flight a non-stop one?

Clerk: Yes, Mr. Green. CA3915 is a non-stop to Shanghai.

Guest: Great, I'll take it!

Clerk: All right. Would you like first class or economy class?

Guest: Economy class.

Clerk: And a window seat or an aisle seat?

Guest: A window seat, please. How much is it?

Clerk: 950 yuan, including the airport construction fee. Would you pay in cash or by credit card?

Guest: By credit card.

Answers:

Booking Tickets
Flight Details
Flight number <u>CA3915</u>　　　　　　Ticket number <u>one</u>
Departure date <u>November 25th</u>　　Departure time <u>8 o'clock a.m.</u>
Destination <u>Shanghai</u>　　　　　　Total Price <u>950 yuan</u>
Flight Class
(　) first class　　　(　) business class　　(√) economy class
Seat
(√) window seat　　(　) middle seat　　　(　) aisle seat
Terms of Payment
(　) pay in cash　　(√) by credit card

book a flight to Shanghai, Which flight do you prefer, a non-stop one, Would you like first class or economy class

III. Exercise

Translations:

1. I'd like to copy this material.

2. Each one A4 costs one yuan.

3. Can you make it a little darker?

4. Is there a fax for me?

5. I need to send a fax to San Francisco.

6. I would like to book a flight to Shanghai next Wednesday.

7. Would you like first class or economy class?

8. Is the morning flight a non-stop one?

Discussion: 略

Travel the Web: 略

Scene Three	Providing Information 提供信息

I. Brainstorm Answers

Telephone service, secretarial services, sightseeing suggestions, delivery service, etc.

II. Warm Up

Buildings:

a. police station (警察局): local office of a police force in a particular area.

b. shopping center (商场): a shopping place for customers with interconnecting walkways that enable customers to walk from unit to unit.

c. supermarket (超市) : a large form of the traditional grocery store, which is a self-service shop offering a wide variety of food and household products, organized into aisles.

d. post office (邮局): a building where you can buy stamps, post letters and packages.

e. bank (银行): an institution where people or businesses can keep their money.

f. drug store (药店): a place where one can buy medicine.

g. library (图书馆): a building where things such as books, newspapers, videos, and music are kept for people to read, use, or borrow.

h. hospital (医院): a place where people who are ill are looked after by nurses and doctors.

i. underground station(地铁站): an underground station or subway station is a railway station for a rapid transit system, often known by names such as "metro","underground" and "subway".

j. bus station (汽车站): a terminal that serves bus passengers.

k. airport (飞机场): a place where aircraft land and take off.

l. railway station (火车站): terminal where trains load or unload passengers or goods.

Task 1:

Dialogue-Scripts:

G: Good morning, this is my first time to Nanjing. Could you please recommend some places of interest in Nanjing?

C: Yes. There are many places such as Dr. Sun Yat-sen's Mausoleum, Confucius Temple and Xuanwu Lake.

G: Err, I've heard of Dr. Sun Yat-sen for ages. He is a great man who devoted his life to pursuing his dream to build a progressive and democratic Republic of China.

C: Right. You're knowledgeable. Dr. Sun Yat-sen's Mausoleum is the most favored highlight among all the historical and cultural attractions in Nanjing.

G: What about the Confucius Temple?

C: It's an ideal place for tourists to understand traditional Chinese culture as well as shopping.

G: Good. Could you give me some information about the Xuanwu Lake?

C: Xuanwu Lake is beautiful with its water and colorful mountains. You can enjoy temples, pavilions and gardens. It's a wonderful place worth visiting.

G: Thanks for your information.

C: You're welcome.

Answers:

Scenic spots in Nanjing	Introduction
Dr. Sun Yatsen's Mausoleum	The most favored highlight among all the historical and cultural attractions in Nanjing.
Confucius Temple	An ideal place for tourists to understand traditional Chinese culture as well as shopping.
Xuanwu Lake	Beautiful with its water and colorful mountains and a wonderful place worth visiting.

Practice: 略

Task 2:

Dialogue-Scripts:

C: Good afternoon. Can I help you?

G: Good afternoon. I'd like to visit night market. Can you recommend me some?

C: Yes. The night market at the Confucius Temple and the night market at Hunan Road are quite famous.

G: Can you give me a brief introduction about these two night markets?

C: Hunan Road night market is a great place to walk in the evening. It has great food, clothing stores, entertainment, and a public park attached at the end while the night market at the Confucius Temple provides the ultimate experience of Chinese folklore, especially around any Chinese festivals. It's a great choice for an after-dinner walk.

G: It's around the New Year's Eve. I'll choose to go to Confucius Temple night market to experience Chinese tradition. Is it far from here? Can you tell me how to go there?

C: It's only 10-minute walk from here. Just go along the street, turn right at the traffic lights and you will see it.

Answers:

visit night market, famous, a brief introduction, a great place to walk, while, Chinese festivals, New Year's Eve, experience Chinese tradition, traffic lights

Task 3:

Dialogue-Scripts:

Clerk(C): Good afternoon, sir. Can I help you?

Mr. Green (G): Good afternoon. Can I post this letter to Los Angeles?

C: Yes, sir. Have you written your return address on the envelope?

G: Yes, I have.

C: Do you want to send it by airmail or by surface mail?

G: By air.

C: Is there anything else in the envelope?

G: Yes, there are some photos in it. How much does it cost by airmail?

R: It depends on the weight. (weighing on the scales) Err ... It's five grams overweight. Do you want it insured?

G: Yes, I'd like to insure it for $50.

R: It will be $15 altogether.

G: Okay. By the way, how long will it take to get there?

R: About five days. Please paste this "AIR MAIL" sticker on the envelope when you send it.

G: Okay, thank you.

C: Is there anything else?

G: Yes, I'd like to buy 8 landscape postcards. How much do they cost?

C: Okay, 8 cards will be $10. The total bill for the letter and the postcards is $25.

Answers:

Mail Service Information
Mail Details
Items mailed: letter, photo
Destination: Los Angeles
Overweight: five grams overweight
Postage of letter: $15
Total bill: $25
Way of mail: by airs

1. post this lestter
2. airmail
3. Is there anything else
4. depends on the weight
5. insure
6. paste

III. Exercise

Translations:

1. Confucius Temple is an ideal place for tourists to understand traditional Chinese

culture as well as shopping.

2. Could you please recommend some places of interest in Nanjing?
3. How much does it cost by airmail?
4. It's five grams overweight.
5. Please paste this "AIR MAIL" sticker on the envelope.
6. Do you want it insured?
7. Can you tell me how to go there?
8. Can you give me a brief introduction about these two night markets?

Discussion: 略

Role-play: 略

Part 6　Special Services　特殊服务英语

Scene One　Recreation Service　康乐服务

I. Brainstorm Answers

Physical exercise, sauna, massage, fitness center, beauty salon, swimming pool, tennis court, table tennis

II. Warm Up

Recreational places or services:

a. bowling alley (保龄球馆):a building which contains several tracks for bowling.

b. golf court (高尔夫球场): a place to play golf.

c. squash court (壁球馆): the indoor court in which squash is played.

d. beauty salon (美容院): a shop where hairdressers and beauticians work.

e. sauna (桑拿房): a small room or building designed to experience dry or wet heat sessions.

f. card room (棋牌室): a gaming establishment that exclusively offers card games for play by the public.

g. fitness center (健身中心): a place housing exercise equipment for the purpose of physical exercise.

h. billiards room (台球室): a recreation room with a billiards table.

i. tennis court (网球场): the court on which tennis is played.

j. Karaoke (卡拉 OK): a form of entertainment in which a machine plays the tunes of songs, and people take it in turns to sing the words.

k. massage (按摩): action of squeezing and rubbing someone's body.

l. pedicure (足疗): care for one's feet by cutting and shaping the nails, etc.

Task 1:

Dialogue-Scripts:

C: Recreation department. Can I help you?

G: Yes. I'd like to do some physical exercise. Would you please give me some information on your facilities?

C: We offer a wide array of recreation facilities and activities to enhance wellness, fitness or release stress. We have a fitness center, a bowling room, a tennis court, an indoor swimming pool and so on.

G: Good. I'm interested in swimming. How is the swimming pool?

C: Our swimming pool is 30-yard with 6-lane and it's free for registered guests.

G: Fantastic. How about the fitness center? Could you tell me what facilities you have?

C: Well, our fitness center is well-equipped with the latest recreational sports apparatus, such as cardio and weight equipment, bar bells, chest expander, stationary bikes that sort of thing.

G: Is there a coach who can provide instruction or help?

C: Yes, of course. Besides, we have full-service locker rooms with showers and saunas near the fitness center.

G: Good. I see. Thank you for your information.

Answers:

a. He wants to know some information on the hotel's facilities.

b. They have a fitness center, a bowling room, a tennis court, an indoor swimming pool and so on.

c. No, it's free.

d. The swimming pool is 30-yard with 6-lane.

e. The fitness center is well-equipped with the latest recreational sports apparatus, such as cardio and weight equipment, bar bells, chest expander, stationary bikes that sort of thing.

Practice:

physical exercise, a wide array of, release stress, interested in, registered guests, fitness center, sort of thing, provide

Task 2:

Dialogue-Scripts:

A: Good evening, sir. Welcome.

G: Good evening. It is said sauna can increase blood circulation, reduce tension and make people relaxed. I'd like to have a try, but I've never experienced before. Could you please tell me something about that?

A: Certainly, sir. We provide dry sauna and steam rooms. As it's your first time to have sauna, you may choose dry sauna as steam room is so humid that you may feel uncomfortable.

G: Great! I'll choose dry sauna. How long does it take?

A: Generally speaking, you can stay as long as you like. However, too long is not good for you.

G: How about half an hour?

A: It's okay. Regular visitors usually spend 45 minutes.

G: What is the temperature in sauna room?

A: It's about 85 degrees centigrade.

G: Good. Now I know what to do. Thank you.

A: You're welcome. When you finish your sauna, you can take a massage.

G: Okay, thank you very much.

Answers:

increase blood circulation, have a try, provide, Generally speaking, Regular visitors, sauna room, take a massage

Practice: 略

Task 3:

Dialogue-Scripts:

S: Good afternoon, sir. Can I be of any assistance?

G: Yes, I'd like to buy some Nanjing specialty for my friends.

S: This way, please. They're all here. We have a great variety of goods for you to choose from. Please look around.

G: What's this? It's so beautiful.

S: It's Yunjin or Nanjing cloud-pattern brocade. It is one of the three brocades well-known in China and abroad and it is a traditional handicraft in China.

G: Wonderful. I'd like to buy some for my wife. I'm sure she will like it. What are these stones?

S: They are Yuhua Stones, one of the most famous handicrafts in Nanjing.

G: Great. I'll choose some for my children. They love stones. Besides, can you recommend some Nanjing specialty food for me?

S: Salty Duck is Nanjing's specialty. What about these bagged salty ducks? It's delicious and easy to take.

G: Thank you. Can you ship the things to America?

S: Certainly, sir. We have a very efficient shipping system. We can pack and ship everything for you.

G: That's very nice.

Answers:

1. F　　2. T　　3. F　　4. T　　5. T　　6. F

Practice:

Nanjing specialty, a great variety of goods, traditional handicraft, recommend some Nanjing specialty food, ship the things to America

III. Exercise

Translations:

1. Our fitness center is well-equipped with the latest recreational sports apparatus.
2. We offer a wide array of recreation facilities and activities to enhance wellness, fitness or release stress.
3. Would you please give me some information on your facilities?
4. I'd like to buy some Nanjing specialty for my friends.
5. We have a great variety of goods for you to choose from.
6. Can you recommend some Nanjing specialty food for me?
7. It is said sauna can increase blood circulation, reduce tension and make people relaxed.
8. When you finish your sauna, you can take a massage.

Oral practice: 略

Role-play: 略

Scene Two	At the Cloakroom　寄存服务

I. Brainstorm Answers

Breakable, valuable, and dangerous items cannot be deposited in the cloakroom.

II. Warm Up

Luggage deposit:

a. luggage deposit slip（行李寄存单）: a small written form that is sometimes used to store your luggage.
b. luggage room（行李房）: a room where baggage or parcels are checked.

c. password locker (密码箱): a suitcase needing password to open.

d. handbag (女用手提包): a bag used for carrying money and small personal items or accessories (especially by women).

e. checked luggage (托运行李): luggage delivered to an airline or train for transportation in the hold of an aircraft or baggage car of a passenger train.

f. bellman of cloakroom (寄存处服务员): a person who works at the luggage deposit office.

g. luggage tag (行李标签): a small piece of card which is attached to luggage.

h. luggage storage tag (行李寄存牌): a piece of wood, metal, or plastic which is given to you when you store your luggage.

i. luggage locker (行李寄存柜): a small cupboard with a lock, where you can put your personal possessions.

j. safety deposit box (保险柜): an individually-secured container.

k. notice (告示牌): a written announcement in a place where everyone can read it.

l. sign (指示牌): a piece of wood, metal, or plastic with words or pictures on it.

Task 1:

Dialogue-Scripts:

Concierge(C)   Guest(G)

C: Good evening, sir. Can I help you?

G: I'm going to check out tomorrow morning. Can I store my luggage in the hotel after check-out? I won't travel back until the day after tomorrow, that is December 10.

C: Certainly. You can store your luggage with us without any extra charges. We offer two kinds of luggage storage service, short term luggage storage and long term luggage storage. How many pieces of luggage will you leave here?

G: A rolling suitcase and a traveling bag, altogether 2 pieces.

C: Are there any valuables or breakables in them?

G: Yes. My laptop, some cash and my passport.

C: Would you mind storing your valuables and breakables in the safety deposit box?

G: No problem. I will take them out. Thanks for your suggestion.

C: Would you show me your room card?

G: Here you are.

C: Tome Green, room 1018, can I have your mobile phone number?

G: My cell phone number is 12340056789.

C: Okay, and you'd like to collect them on December 10th, am I right?

G: Yes.

C: Mr. Green, would you please sign your name here on the luggage deposit slip?

G: Okay. Here you are.

C: Thank you, Mr. Green. Here's your receipt. Please show it when you come to claim your luggage.

G: Okay. Thank you.

```
┌──────────────────────────────────────────────────────────────────┐
│                          Luggage Deposit                           │
│ Guest Details                                                      │
│ Name: Tome Green                                                   │
│ Room No.: Room 1018                                                │
│ Phone: 12340056789                                                 │
│ Deposit details                                                    │
│ Piece of  luggage   2 pieces                                       │
│ Date for depositing December 8 (D/M/Y)                             │
│ Date for drawing back December 10 (D/M/Y)                          │
│ Guest's signature_____      Date _____           │
│ Concierge's signature_____   Date _____          │
└──────────────────────────────────────────────────────────────────┘
```

Answers:

check out, the day after tomorrow, luggage storage service, valuables and breakables, room card, collect, luggage deposit slip, claim

Task 2:

Dialogue-Scripts:

G: Good evening, I'd like to pick up my luggage.

C: May I have your luggage tag, please?

G: I'm awfully sorry. I tried to find it for a long time, but I failed. I've lost my tag. What should I do?

C: Take it easy, sir. Do you remember your tag number?

G: Yes, No. 23, and here is my ID card.

C: How many pieces have you got? Can you describe the features of your baggage?

G: Uh, two pieces. One is a green suitcase with two wheels and the other is a grey backpack.

C: Are these yours, sir?

G: Yes. Thank you very much.

C: You're welcome, Mr. Green.

Answers:

a. No, he lost it.

b. No. 23.

c. Two pieces.

d. One is a green suitcase with two wheels and the other is a grey backpack.

Task 3:

Dialogue-Scripts:

C: Good afternoon, madam. Can I help you?

G: Yes, I was wondering whether I can deposit my laptop, tickets and some cash here.

C: Of course, madam. We provide safety deposit boxes for our registered guests to store valuables. You can deposit the valuables in the hotel's safe deposit box. Could you show me your room card and your identification or passport?

G: Here you are.

C: Yeah, Ms. Green. Please put your tickets and cash in this envelope, seal it and sign on it.

G: No problem. Is it free?

C: Yes, it's free for our registered guests. Would you please fill out this safe deposit application form?

G: All right.

C: This way, please, Ms. Green. Your box number is 18.

Answers:

a. Laptop, tickets and some cash.

b. Safety deposit box.

c. Yes.

d. Envelope.

e. Room card and identification or passport.

Practice:

whether I can, safety deposit boxes, deposit the valuables, tickets and cash, application form

III. Exercise

Translations:

1. Would you please sign your name here on the luggage deposit slip?

2. How many pieces of luggage will you leave here?

3. Are there any valuables or breakables in it?

4. I'd like to pick up my luggage.

5. You can deposit the valuables in the hotel's safe deposit box.

6. Would you please fill out this safe deposit application form?

7. We provide safety deposit box for our registered guests.

8. We offer two kinds of luggage storage service, short term luggage storage and long term luggage storage.

Dialogue-Scripts:

G: Excuse me, where can I deposit my luggage?

R: Yes, madam. You can check your luggage here.

G: Good, what should I do?

R: May I have your name and room number?

G: Yes, room 1008.

R: Ms. Green, how many pieces of luggage do you have?

G: Three pieces altogether.

R: When will you want it?

G: In two days.

R: Is there any breakable or valuable in the luggage?

G: No. There isn't.

R: Ms. Green, here is your luggage check card. Please keep it, you need to show it when you come to pick up your luggage.

Answers:

1, 6, 2, 5, 3, 7, 12, 8, 4, 9, 10, 11

Role-play: 略

Scene Three　　　　Handling Complaints　处理投诉

I. Brainstorm Answers

Complaint about poor service, facilities or products, sanitary conditions and abnormal cases, miscalculation, luggage delay, mis-delivery, equipment in room such as air conditioner, TV, minibar, dirty bedcover, slow service, wrong food delivery, poor quality of food, etc.

II. Warm Up

Complaints-handling:

a. listening (聆听): the act of hearing attentively.

b. apology (道歉): an expression of regret at having caused trouble for someone.

c. understanding (理解): an inclination to support or be loyal to or to agree with an opinion.

d. communication (沟通): the activity of conveying information.

e. handling complaint (处理投诉): dealing with complaint.

f. feedback (反馈): response to an inquiry.

g. Complaints Department (投诉处): places to deal with complaints.

h. ways of complaints (投诉方式): channels to complain.

i. steps to deal with complaints (处理投诉步骤): steps to solve complaints.

j. food complaint (餐饮投诉): complaining about food.

k. complaint letter (投诉信): a letter statement in which you express your dissatisfaction with a particular situation.

l. room complaint (客房投诉): complaining about room.

Task 1:

Dialogue-Scripts:

S: Staff   G: Guest

S: Good afternoon, Front office. What can I do for you?

G: Good afternoon. This is Mr. Green from Room 902. I have just checked in and I'm not happy with my room. Can you change the room for me?

S: I'm really sorry, sir. May I know what is wrong?

G: The bedspread is not clean and there is hair on the bed! I couldn't bear it.

S: I'm awfully sorry to hear that, Mr. Green. We might overlook some points. That is our responsibility. I'll arrange another comfortable room for you at once.

G: By the way, the room is close to the elevator so it is always noisy, would you please change a quiet room for me?

S: Certainly, sir. We'll manage it. The bellman will come to carry your luggage to room 912 which is at the end of the corridor. We do apologize for the inconvenience.

G: All right. I hope I'll be able to enjoy my stay in a quiet suite and have a sound sleep.

S: Be sure. And if there is anything more you need, please let us know. Please accept my apology on behalf of the hotel. I assure you we will make every effort to make your evening here a pleasant one.

Answers:

> **Guest's name:** Mr. Green
> **Room No.:** Room 902
> **Complaint:** The bedspread is not clean and there is hair on the bed.
> The room is close to the elevator and it is always noisy.
> **Solution:** change the room.

Practice:

change the room, bedspread, overlook, arrange another comfortable room, manage it, apologize, on behalf of

Task 2: 略

Task 3:

Dialogue-Scripts:

R: Good afternoon, sir. Welcome to our hotel. Can I help you?

G: Yes, please. I'm Tom Green. I have reserved two double rooms a week ago.

R: Err ... Mr. Green. Let me check. Is the reservation made under you?

G: Yes, here is the confirmation notice.

R: I'm sorry there must be some mistake. There is no reservation record.

G: No record? Impossible! I have the confirmation notice.

R: I do apologize. There must be something wrong, but we have no double room available now. How about other rooms?

G: I'm so disappointed with your hotel. I just need what I have reserved.

R: Mr. Green, would you please wait a moment? I'll call the manager to ask for his advice.

G: Go ahead.

M: Good afternoon, Mr. Green, I'm the manager. Sorry to bring you inconvenience. There's a suite available. Would that be ok?

G: Well, what's the rate?

M: Well, to express our regret for all the trouble, we'd like to offer you a 20% discount. In fact, it's the same price as what you have reserved.

G: It seems reasonable.

M: Mr. Green, I hope you can enjoy your stay here. If you need any help, don't hesitate to call us. We're always at your service.

Answers:

1. F 2. F 3. T 4. T 5. F

Practice:

Is the reservation made under you，reservation record, disappointed with your hotel, call the manager, 20% discount

III. Exercise

Translations:

1. The bedspread is not clean and there is hair on the bed!

2. That is our responsibility.

3. I'll arrange another comfortable room for you at once.

4. We do apologize for the inconvenience.

5. I'm sorry there must be some mistake.

6. I'll call the manager to ask for his advice.

7. There's a suite available. Would that be ok?

8. To express our regret for all the trouble, we'd like to offer you a 20% discount.

Order: 7, 3, 1, 6, 2, 4, 5

Discussion: 略

Appendix
附　　录

Appendix I
Hotel Management Organization
酒店管理人员岗位英文名称

Board of Directors 董事会

General Manager (G.M.) 总经理
Deputy G.M. 副总经理
Hotel Manager 驻店经理

Sales & Marketing Director 市场营销总监

Executive Office 总经理办公室
Group Sales Manager 团队销售经理
Commercial Sales Manager 商务销售经理
Public Relations Manager 公关部经理
Senior Sales Executive 高级销售代表
Planning Manager 策划经理

Hr Director 人力资源总监

Personnel Manager 人事部经理
Training Manager 培训部经理
Quality Inspector 督导部经理

Controller Director 财务总监

Deputy Controller 计财副总监
Accountign Manager 财务部经理
Chief Accountant 总出纳
Cost Department Manager 成本部经理
Purchasing Manager 采购部经理
Purchasing Officer 采购部主管
Storeroom Officer 仓库主管
I.S. Manager 电脑部经理

Room Director 房务总监

Front Office Manager 前厅部经理
Assistant Manager 大堂副理
Chief Concierge 礼宾部经理
Executive Housekeeper 行政管家

Laundry Manager 洗衣房经理
Business Center Manager 商务中心经理
Floor Manager 楼层主管

F & B Director 餐饮总监

Deputy F&B Director 餐饮副总监
Executive Sous Chef 行政主厨
W. Kitchen Sous Chef 西厨厨师长
C. Kitchen Sous Chef 中厨厨师长
Catering Manager 宴会部经理
F&B Manager 餐饮部经理

Recreation Director 康乐总监

Entertainment Manager 娱乐部经理
Recreation Center Supervisor 康乐主管
Shopping Center Manager 商场部经理

Security Director 行政保卫总监

Administration Manager 行政部经理
Security Manager 保卫部经理
Engineering Manager 工程部经理
Chief Engineer 工程总监

Appendix II
Food & Beverage Vocabulary   餐饮常用词汇

Cooking Method 烹调方式			
fry 煎	steam 蒸	braise 炖	stew 煨
stir-fry 爆炒	smoke 熏	roast 烤	toffee 拔丝
mashed 泥、馅	dices 丁	shreds 丝	cubes 块
slices 片	in brown sauce 红烧	with fish flavor 鱼香	with sweet and sour flavor 糖醋

Condiments 调味品			
salt 食盐	sugar 白糖	vinegar 醋	soy sauce 酱油
pepper 胡椒	curry 咖喱	honey 蜂蜜	mustard 芥茉
cheese 奶酪/干酪	butter 黄油	cream 奶油	gravy 肉汁
jam 果酱	tomato sauce 番茄酱	mayonnaise 蛋黄酱	sweet soybean paste 甜面酱

Soup 汤			
thin soup 清汤	thick soup 浓汤	vegetable soup 蔬菜汤	tomato soup 西红柿汤
hot and sour soup 酸辣汤	beef soup 牛肉汤	chicken soup 鸡汤	creamed prawn soup 奶油虾汤

Chinese Food 中餐			
steamed bun 馒头	steamed twisted roll 花卷	pancake 煎饼	egg fried rice 蛋炒饭
meat bun 包子	dumpling 饺子	meat pie 馅饼	wonton 馄饨
noodles 面条	noodles with soup 汤面	fried noodles 炒面	rice noodles 米线
sweet dumpling 元宵	spring roll 春卷	soybean milk 豆浆	deep-fried dough sticks 油条

Western Food 西餐			
bread 面包	toast 土司	hamburger 汉堡包	sandwich 三明治
hotdog 热狗	pizza 比萨饼	oatmeal 燕麦粥	muffin 松饼
macaroni 通心面	spaghetti 意大利面条	French fries 炸薯条	bagel 硬面包圈

Dessert 甜点			
cream cake 奶油蛋糕	apple pie 苹果馅饼	vanilla ice-cream 香草冰激凌	pudding 布丁
custard tart 蛋挞	puff 泡芙	cookie 曲奇	donut 甜甜圈
mousse 慕斯	tiramisu 提拉米苏	cheese cake 奶酪蛋糕	cupcake 纸杯蛋糕

Drinks 酒水			
white wine 白葡萄酒	red wine 红葡萄酒	sherry 雪利酒	champagne 香槟酒
martini 马丁尼	vermouth 味美思酒	gin 杜松子酒	whisky 威士忌
brandy 白兰地	whiskey 威士忌	vodka 伏特加	rum 朗姆酒
punch 潘趣酒	liquor 利口酒	cider 苹果酒	cocktail 鸡尾酒
black coffee 不加奶咖啡	white coffee 牛奶咖啡	instant coffee 速溶咖啡	plain coffee 纯咖啡
green tea 绿茶	black tea 红茶	jasmine tea 茉莉花茶	tea bags 袋泡茶
yogurt 酸奶	fruit juice 水果汁	mineral water 矿泉水	soda 汽水
coke 可口可乐	7-up 七喜	Pepsi 百事可乐	Sprite 雪碧
lemonade 柠檬汁	beer 啤酒	light beer 淡啤酒	draught beer 生啤
tonic water 汤力水	ginger ale 干姜水	diet coke 无糖可乐	milk shake 奶昔

Fruits 水果			
apple 苹果	apricot 杏	durian 榴梿	lychee 荔枝
mango 杧果	lemon 柠檬	watermelon 西瓜	papaya 木瓜
olive 橄榄	grapefruit 西柚	plum 梅子	peach 桃子
guava 番石榴	strawberry 草莓	blueberry 蓝莓	cranberry 蔓越莓
pineapple 菠萝	grape 葡萄	kiwi fruit 奇异果	longan 龙眼
avocado 牛油果	tangerine 柑橘	pear 梨	cherry 樱桃

参 考 文 献

[1] 袁露，阮蓓，李飞. 酒店英语 [M]. 天津：天津大学出版社，2010.

[2] 胡扬政. 现代酒店服务英语 [M]. 北京：清华大学出版社，2013.

[3] 胡扬政. 酒店英语服务实训 [M]. 北京：清华大学出版社，2010.

[4] 郭兆康. 饭店情景英语 [M]. 上海：复旦大学出版社，2000.

[5] 王艳，胡新莲. 酒店英语 [M]. 重庆：重庆大学出版社，2010.

[6] 王迎新. 酒店英语 [M]. 北京：中国林业大学出版社，2011.

[7] 王艳，任虹. 酒店英语实训教程 [M]. 北京：机械工业出版社，2013.

[8] 蔡丽巍. 酒店岗位英语 [M]. 北京：国防工业出版社，2012.

[9] 魏新民，申延子. 酒店情景英语 [M]. 北京：北京大学出版社，2011.

[10] 朱华. 酒店英语：视听版 [M]. 北京：北京大学出版社，2014.

[11] 江波，李啟金. 酒店实用英语 [M]. 天津：天津大学出版社，2011.

[12] Stott Trish. Highly recommended : English for the hotel and catering industry[M]. Oxford : Oxford University Press, 1994.

[13] Francis O Hara.Be my guest : English for the hotel industry[M]. Cambridge : Cambridge University Press, 2008.

[14] Seymour Mike. Hotel & Hospitality English[M]. London : Collins, 2011.

[15] Talalla, Renee. Main Course : language and skills for restaurant workers[M]. Selangor Malaysia: Falcon Press, 2000.

[16] Harding Keith. High Season : English for the Hotel and Tourist Industry[M]. Oxford: Oxford University Press,1994.

[17] Practical English For U.S. Restaurant, Times Publishing (NY) ltd.

推 荐 阅 读

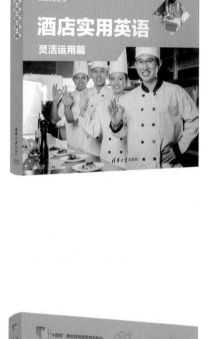

《酒店实用英语（灵活运用篇）》

本书主要针对培养酒店、旅游专业学生或酒店服务人员的英语听说能力以及在实际工作岗位上的英语运用能力，突出行业外语的应用能力培养。本书内容真实还原了工作本来面貌，注重以实际工作流程为导向，同时紧扣《酒店运营管理职业技能等级证书》。本系列教材贯彻党的二十大精神，内容融入中国特色思政元素，方便一线教师教学使用。书中内容不仅与职业资格证书挂钩、与行业接轨，实现分层次培养人才的目的，而且密切结合酒店前厅、客房、餐饮等岗位群的典型工作任务，突出现代旅游服务业从业人员的英语语言表达、人际交往、沟通协调和应变能力等综合素质的培养。

《酒店实用英语（基础会话篇）》

《酒店实用英语(基础会话篇)》针对酒店英语初级学习者编写。本系列教材内容体系以实际工作流程为导向，让学生自然融入真实情境，实现掌握职业英语的目的。同时贯彻党的二十大精神，巧妙融入中国特色思政元素，真正让学习入脑入心。本书紧扣《酒店运营管理职业技能等级证书》，共有6个模块、20个主题情境和60个子任务；学习内容以完成任务、解决问题入手，侧重听说训练及课堂小组讨论，配有课件和音频二维码，体现职业性、实用性、趣味性和时代感。既适合高职高专酒店管理专业学生的实践教学使用，也可作为酒店行业一线员工培训教材和自学读本，还适合"一带一路"沿线国家在华留学生酒店管理课程学习使用。